EXPLORING THE FUTURE
OF MISSION IN AFRICA

In Celebration of Maryknoll's
100 Years in Mission

Editors
Laurenti Magesa
Michael C. Kirwen

MIAS BOOKS

Nairobi, Kenya

ISBN 9789966-7126-3-1

Library of Congress cataloging-in-Publication Data

Queries regarding rights and permissions should be addressed to:
Maryknoll Institute of African Studies,
P.O. Box 15199
00509, Lang'ata
Kenya.

Printed in Kenya

Exploring the Future of Mission in Africa

In Celebration of Maryknoll's 100 Years in Mission

Editors
Laurenti Magesa
Michael C. Kirwen

The Catholic Foreign Missionary Society of America, popularly known as the Maryknoll Fathers and Brothers, was founded in 1911. The Maryknoll Sisters in 1912.

The Maryknoll Missionaries include Priests, Brothers, Sisters, Lay Missionaries, Affiliates and Volunteers.

As of April 2011 there were seventy-eight Missionaries in the Maryknoll Family in Africa: thirty members of Maryknoll Society (twenty-six priests and four brothers) of whom eleven serve in Kenya, thirty-three Maryknoll Sisters (of whom four serve in Kenya); and fifteen Maryknoll Lay Missioners (of whom ten serve in Kenya).

Worldwide there are a total of nine hundred and sixty-four Maryknollers; four hundred and thirteen Maryknoll Fathers and Brothers, four hundred and ninety eight Maryknoll Sisters and fifty three Lay Missioners.

Maryknoll Society
P. O. Box 43058, 00100
Nairobi, Kenya
website-http://www.maryknollafrica.org

Copies are available at the following address
P. O. Box 15199, 00509, Lang'ata, Nairobi, Kenya.
Website: http://www.africancultures.org

Cell phone: (254)732-818-917 or (254)726-818- 917
Email: miasmu@tangaza.org

DEDICATION

To the hundreds of Maryknoll
Priests, Brothers, Sisters, Lay Missionaries, Affiliates
and Volunteers, many of whom are now deceased,
who were assigned to Mission in Africa
since 1946

Table of Contents

Preface--i

Forward -- iii

Acknowledgements---vii

Introduction--- 1

Part I: Mission to Justice --- 5

    Greetings: Ms. Mary Oldham, MLM---------------------------------- 5

    Tangaza College Congratulates Maryknoll on its
Centenary Celebrations--- 7

    Africans In Global Mission -- 9

    Does the Church have a Role in Economic Justice? -----------------15

    Break-out Discussion Group Report on Economic Justice ---------27

    Discovering the Role of the Church in the Protection of Civilians
in Peace Support Operations---29

    Break-out Discussion Group on Peace Building --------------------45

    Mission to Justice from a Healthcare Perspective -------------------47

    The Environment and the Integrity of Creation ----------------------55

    Break-out Discussion Group Report on the Environment and
Integrity of Creation ---63

Part II: Mission "ad Gentes" --67

Greetings: Sister Teresa Hougnon, MM -----------------------------67

A Christian among Moslems---69

Break-out Discussion Group on Inter-religious Dialogue -----------77

Christian Presence among Marginalized Groups
in Northern Kenya--81

Break-out Discussion Group Report on Evangelization in the
Marginalized Communities in Northern Kenya ----------------------93

Theology of Mission --95

Break-out Discussion Group on Theology of Mission ------------ 117

Part III: Theological Reflections------------------------------- 119

Greetings: Rev. Joseph Healey, MM------------------------------- 119

Theological Reflections on the Future of Mission in Africa ------ 121

The Quest for Holistic Mission------------------------------------- 135

The Credibility of the Church doing Mission in Africa ----------- 149

Part IV: Concluding Remarks -------------------------------- 161

His Grace Archbishop Allan Lebeaupin,
The Apostolic Nuncio to Kenya ----------------------------------- 161

Rev. Paul R. Masson, MM -- 165

Most Rev. Boniface Lele --- 167

Contributors -- 169

Preface

Rev. Joseph Healey, MM

Throughout this calendar year 2011 the Maryknoll Society of Fathers and Brothers is celebrating its 100th Anniversary as a global missionary society (1911-2011) and 65 years of missionary service in Africa (1946-2011). To highlight mission we are celebrating a wide variety of masses, meetings, seminars, talks, meals and social activities. We wanted to sponsor one event to focus on the theological and pastoral dimensions of mission on a deeper level. This book documents the proceedings of "The Future of Mission in Africa: 100th Anniversary Symposium 2011" that took place at Tangaza College in Nairobi, Kenya on 1-2 April, 2011.

The themes of our symposium reflected a contemporary reading of the signs of the times in Africa including two paradigm shifts in mission. On the first day the Panel Presentations were on "Mission to Justice" with Breakout Discussion Groups on the various topics. In Maryknoll's 65 years in Africa we have seen the content of mission shift from Parish Pastoral Work to Development Work to Inculturation, Presence, Witness and Justice. On the second day the Panel Presentations were on "Mission ad Gentes (to the Nations)" with Breakout Discussion Groups on the various topics. We have seen the personnel of mission shift from missionaries coming to Africa from the Global North such as we American missionaries mainly priests, brothers and sisters to missionaries from the Global South – African missionaries going to other parts of Africa and throughout the world. So the focus today is not on the role of expatriate missionaries, but African missionaries both within Africa and outside Africa. This shift includes two aspects. First, in this process we missionaries are evangelized by the African people. Second, the African missionaries of the future will be more and more lay missionaries.

This mission symposium has focused on the pastoral rather than the academic. How are we mission evangelizers? How and where and for what are we "sent" (the very meaning of mission)? The closing ceremony led by Archbishop Boniface Lele used the theme of 2011 World Mission Sunday on 23 October, 2011: "As the Father sends me I send you" (John 20-21). Jesus Christ continues to send us today in mission. We are messengers of the Good News of Jesus Christ to all peoples and in all situations.

Rev. Joseph Healey, M.M. is considered one of the leading researchers, compilers and writers on African Proverbs, Sayings and Stories. He is the Moderator of the African Proverbs, Sayings and Stories Website at http://www.afriprov.org and the Networking Coordinator of the Small Christian Communities Global Collaborative Website at http://www.smallchristiancommunities.org. He has worked in Kenya for many years.

Foreword

Rev. Lance Nadeau, MM

As part of the centennial celebrations of the Catholic Foreign Mission Society of America, the Maryknoll Fathers and Brothers in Africa invited scholars and active missioners to share their ideas on the future of mission in Africa. The purpose of this gathering was to explore what Africans should be thinking about as they prepare to take a more directive role in global mission. Rather than the future of foreign missionaries in Africa, the symposium was to be a conversation about the future of mission undertaken by African missionaries both within and outside Africa.

A large body of literature in the social sciences and mission studies reads the signs of the times and reports on the striking accelerating shift in the center of Christianity from the global North to the global South. It is unlikely that European and North American churches, missionary institutes, and lay movements will define and implement the mission agenda of the next century. Rather local churches, missionary institutes, and lay movements of the global South will do that. The numbers of missionaries from India and South Korea, the recruitment of southern clergy for US dioceses, and the presence of the Apostles of Jesus in the USA, all indicate a growing southern commitment to mission. Indeed, the new evangelization proposed by John Paul II and Benedict XVI may be the first major work of the new southern missionaries. The Maryknoll Fathers and Brothers in Africa saw our centennial as the right time, the kairos, to look forward to a future of mission that promises to be conspicuously different from the past of mission.

Two major subjects guided the symposium's discussions: "Mission to Justice: 'Seek First the Kingdom of God'" and "Mission ad Gentes: Gathering the Scattered Children of God." The choice of these two themes was in keeping with Maryknoll's century-long promise to seek first the kingdom of God and his/its justice and the Society's commitment to the person's free practice of religion and the inviolability of conscience. "Mission to Justice" guided participants in their reflections on what African missionaries need to know about economic justice, peace-building, environmental issues, and medical ministry. "Mission ad Gentes," led the gathering to explore what African missionaries need to know about interreligious dialogue, Christian presence among marginalized groups, and some important theological aspects of mission ad gentes. This volume offers the reader the major papers that spurred discussion among the symposium's participants.

In the gospel of Matthew Jesus offers this arresting comparison, with its unexpected, unnatural order of new and old: "Every scribe who has been discipled for the kingdom of heaven is like the owner of a house who brings out of his treasure what is new and old" (13:52). Undoubtedly, African missioners will in the future draw on the old treasures of the "single but complex and articulated reality" of mission: "the simple presence and living witness of the Christian life … the service of humankind and all forms of activity for social development and the struggle against poverty and the structures which produce it … liturgical life … prayer and contemplation … dialogue in which Christians meet the followers of other religious traditions … announcement and catechesis (Dialogue and Mission, 13).

But they will not merely repeat the past, to which Maryknoll has contributed so effectively. Alongside the old, African missioners — we trust — will in the future bring forth the new, which provides the key to appropriating the past. They will present the old in a new light; they will reclaim it for the new situations, the "new things" of God (Isa 42:9), in which the human family will find itself; they will see the groaning creation (Rom 8:22-23) in the light of the Messiah who disciples us through his cross and resurrection; they will bring forward into our time the promised heavens and new earth.

Rev. Lance Nadeau, M.M. is currently the Regional Superior for Maryknoll Fathers and Brothers, Africa Region. He also serves as the Catholic Chaplain at Kenyatta University for the last 8 years.

Acknowledgments

The success of the symposium and the publishing of this book would not have been but for the selfless efforts of many people. Just to mention a few, the General Council of Maryknoll Fathers and Brothers, the Regional Superior, Rev. Lance Nadeau, MM, the organizing committee led by Rev. Joseph Healey, MM, the editors, Rev. Laurenti Magesa and Rev. Michael Kirwen, MM, the MIAS BOOKS editorial staff - Ms. Edith Chamwama and Betty Kiema, all the contributors to the book, all those who attended the symposium, and the staff at Maryknoll Institute of African Studies, Tangaza College.

Asanteni!

Introduction

Rev. Laurenti Magesa

Mission is understood in a more comprehensive sense today than was the case only a few decades ago. Doing mission or being on or in mission includes, of course, the more traditional and strictly theological sense of verbally preaching the gospel "to all nations" so as to get people to accept baptism and thereby become visible members of the church. But mission in our era is seen to go beyond this narrow definition and entails involvement in social, economic, and political issues as essential aspects of it wherever the church finds itself. Concern about justice, peace, and reconciliation within and among nations, for example, or good governance, health matters, education, freedom, human rights, liberation, and interreligious dialogue, and so on, now forms an integral part of the understanding and practice of the mission of the church. All of these aspects are a "constitutive" part of preaching the gospel, the call to human salvation.

No missionary organization in Africa has epitomized this new understanding of mission in a very visible and sustained way better than the Foreign Mission Society of America, otherwise known as the Maryknoll Fathers and Brothers or simply Maryknoll. In their 65 years of presence in Africa, since 1946, the Maryknoll Fathers and Brothers have not only built churches and inducted thousands upon thousands of people into the church wherever they have been – thus fulfilling to the letter the mandate to proclaim the word to all nations. From the very beginning of their ministry in Africa, they have also built schools, dispensaries and social halls, been involved in social

1

work with women and youth, been seen as advocates of justice and peace among the sick and unlettered, and acted as defenders of the poor and oppressed. (I can personally testify to all of this because, coincidentally, I was born the in the year and at the location they first arrived, and have grown up witnessing their activities there and elsewhere). It is an open secret that in the 1960s and 70s, years marking the struggle for political independence throughout the continent, some Maryknollers were in the forefront of encouraging this struggle by supporting several African leaders to fight for this most fundamental of human rights, and have continued to support the effort in various ways ever since. Later, this work of the Maryknoll Fathers and Brothers was augmented by the able partnership of the Maryknoll Lay Association of the Faithful.

In 2011 the Maryknoll Society celebrated the centenary of its founding (in 1911), with its first missionaries being sent to the Far East. The Society in Africa marked this event by, among other things, holding a symposium with the theme of the future of mission in Africa and beyond. The symposium was held – most appropriately – at Tangaza College, a constituent College of the Catholic University of Eastern Africa. Tangaza is situated in Nairobi, Kenya, in the heart of Africa and is an Institute dedicated to the training and formation of missionaries for Africa and the world. The symposium took place on April 1 – April 2, 2011, and was attended very well by laypeople, religious men and women, priests, seminarians, people in various professions, social workers, medical personnel, and theologians. A bishop friend of Maryknoll and the Papal Representative in Kenya also spoke at this symposium. Interest in the proceedings was visibly high, a clear recognition, in my opinion, of the achievement of Maryknoll in mission in Africa.

This book contains the complete record of the proceedings of this symposium, the messages given, the papers presented and the conclusions of the discussion groups over the two or so days of deliberations. They make very inspiring reading, especially in the light of the second African Synod and the Holy Father's recent Apostolic Exhortation, Africae Munus, promulgated in Benin in November 2011. The book is especially significant and useful because it looks not to the past but to the future. It addresses the practical question: How should we do mission in the 21st century? For evangelizers in the African church the book seems to me to be indispensable because it contains reflections not by theoreticians but by people who are practically and currently engaged in the different dimensions of evangelization as pastors, social workers, teachers, volunteers, and conversation partners with members of African Religion and Islam. These are the situations of evangelization the church faces in Africa; these are the issues this book sheds much needed light on. This is why it is a pleasure and an honor for me to have had the privilege of editing it and now presenting it to you, the reader, for reflection and action.

Rev. Prof. Laurenti Magesa is a priest of the Catholic Diocese of Musoma, Tanzania. He holds a Ph.D. and D.Th. in Moral Theology earned at St. Paul University, Ottawa, Canada. He is an Associate Professor of Saint Mary's University of Minnesota, MN/USA attached to the Maryknoll Institute of African Studies, which is located on its Nairobi Campus. He has taught in many institutions of higher learning such as The Maryknoll Institute of African Studies, Nairobi, Campus since 1989, the Catholic University of Eastern Africa (CUEA), the Maryknoll School of Theology, New York and Xavier University, Cincinnati, OH, USA. Currently he teaches African Theology at Hekima and Tangaza Colleges in Nairobi. He is also a prolific author.

PART I
MISSION TO JUSTICE

Greetings

Ms. Mary Oldham, MLM

Good afternoon! On behalf of the Maryknoll Family, I would like welcome you to the Future of Mission in Africa Symposium. My name is Mary Oldham, and I am a Maryknoll Lay Missioner. I am honored today to be with you and to represent one of the three branches of the Maryknoll Family, the Maryknoll Lay Missioners. The Maryknoll Fathers and Brothers are celebrating the 100th Anniversary of the founding of Maryknoll, the Foreign Mission Society of America. Next year the Maryknoll Sisters will be celebrating 100 years since their beginning. We would like to thank you for coming to join us as we celebrate the past and look forward to the future of mission in Africa.

This afternoon we will be hearing from Fr Michael Kirwen about Africans in Global Mission as well as a panel discussion on Justice in Mission – with topics ranging from Economics, Peace building, Medicine and the Environment. From there, we will begin our discussion in small groups and end today with our sharing with each other in plenary.

To start our proceedings for today, I would like to introduce Fr. Patrick Roe, the Principal of Tangaza College and a good friend to Maryknoll. Please join me in welcoming him.

Ms. Mary Oldham is a Maryknoll Lay Missioner working in the Catholic Archdiocese of Mombasa. Mary's ministry is working with the HIV and AIDS Orphans Project in Mombasa. The mission of the project is to be a sign of hope to families and especially the children afflicted or affected by HIV and AIDS, showing them that God does care, and has not abandoned them. She has a degree in Chemical Engineering from Iowa State University.

Tangaza College Congratulates Maryknoll on its Centenary Celebrations 2011

Rev. Patrick Roe, CSSp

It is a great pleasure for us at Tangaza College to congratulate the Maryknoll Society on the occasion of your centenary celebrations. We are also proud that the Society chose Tangaza College as the location for the celebrations of your centenary in Kenya. You represent the extraordinary dynamism and genius of the American Church towards world mission, which characterises any Christian Church worthy of the name. It is the occasion for us all to thank God for the fruitfulness in mission growing out of that original Mary's Knoll on the banks of the Hudson, in Ossining, New York, founded in 1911 by your two great founders, Fr. James Anthony Walsh and Fr. Thomas Fredrick Price.

Many parts of Asia and Latin America have good reason to be thankful for the founding of Maryknoll. But particularly we in the East African churches have reason, since 1946, to be thankful for the expansion of Maryknoll into East Africa: initially in Musoma and Shinyanga in Tanzania, later into Kenya, and more recently into Ethiopia, Mozambique, Namibia, South Sudan and Sudan.

I can safely assume that Fr. Walsh, from his name and from his Bostonian origins had an Irish lineage, and he might have understood the Irish proverb: *athníonn ciaróg ciaróg eile*, which literally means an earwig recognises another earwig. Perhaps it is some such mutual

7

recognition which attracted Maryknoll to Tangaza College from the earliest days of the College in 1986. Tangaza as the Swahili word suggests is about proclamation, proclamation of the Good News of Jesus Christ, and therefore acts as a magnet for Societies, Congregations and individuals dedicated to mission.

We are proud of the presence among us of MIASMU (the Maryknoll Institute of African Studies) under the direction of Michael Kirwen, which has done so much for the development of cultural sensitivity and insight, such an essential ingredient for enlightened mission. We thank you for the selfless dedication to mission provided to Tangaza and to the East African Church by Claudette LaVerdiere and Joe Healey. We thank you also for the service of academic and spiritual enlightenment provided to world mission by Orbis Books.

I note with appreciation the words of John Conway, perhaps quoting an earlier Maryknoll source: We come, perhaps, when we are needed but not wanted, because we are unknown. We leave when we are wanted, but not needed. We pray that the Holy Spirit will give the insight, not only to Maryknoll, but to the rest of the missionary societies in Africa to be able to distinguish when they are wanted but not needed.

Rev. Patrick Roe is a member of Holy Ghost Fathers (CSSp). He has a Doctorate in Divinity earned at Maynooth, Ireland. Currently he is the Principal of Tangaza College, Nairobi, Kenya.

Africans in Global Mission

Rev. Michael C. Kirwen, MM

Welcome to all our friends and guests as we celebrate the hundredth anniversary of the Maryknoll Society, together with the Maryknoll Sisters, the Maryknoll Association of the Faithful and the Maryknoll Associates.

Maryknoll was founded by Bishop Anthony Walsh, who was the Society of the Propagation of the Faith (SPS) director from Boston, and Fr. Thomas Price, a diocesan priest from South Carolina. The two met in Montreal, Canada, and together began a project that led to the founding of the Maryknoll Society in 1911. The official name was and is "The Catholic Foreign Mission Society of America." The popular name "Maryknoll" comes from the knoll of land on the farm where they located the society, and since the society was dedicated to Mary, hence Mary's knoll. Its structure followed that of the Paris Foreign Mission Society.

Missions in the Orient

The first missions of Maryknoll were in China, with the first group sent off in 1913. Over time missions were opened in Japan, Taiwan, Korea, and the Philippines. Two of the Maryknoll bishops died for their faith during the war years, one in China, Bishop Ford, and the other, Bishop Bryne, on a death march in North Korea.

It was during the time of the Second World War that Maryknoll turned its attention to Africa and Latin America, and afterwards began to send personnel into those regions. This process was hastened by the closure of China to all foreign missionaries.

Missions in Africa

The first Maryknollers arrived in Africa in 1946 and were assigned to a new diocese of Musoma in Tanzania which had been split off from Mwanza. At the hand-over from the Missionaries of Africa, there were only two parishes in operation in Musoma, Nyegina and Kowak. Some time later another new diocese, Shinyanga, was also cut off from Mwanza and handed over to Maryknoll. The first bishops of both of these dioceses were Maryknoll priests

When I was assigned to Musoma in 1963 there were already nineteen parishes established. However, there were only two ordained African priests. At the peak of its work in the mid-seventies, there were close to 100 Maryknollers assigned to these two dioceses. In Musoma, seven local languages were being used pastorally, and one learned the language depending on one's assignment, while in Shinyanga there was one local language, Kisukuma. It was only in the early eighties, after Kiswahili had been taught as a medium of instruction in the primary and secondary school system, that it could be used pastorally and the study of the local languages went by the board for most.

From the beginning of my residence in Africa, I was struck by how my African colleague were in the same kind of missionary problematic as I when they were assigned to a parish that was located in a ethnic area different than their own. They, of course, were more accustomed to an African life style than I, but they had the same challenges of learning another language and trying to understand and relate to the local people as an adult. So being like missionary was an ordinary reality for the local African clergy – at least in Musoma.

Maryknollers branched out from these original commitments, taking parish assignment in major cities of Tanzania, moving to Kenya and building five parishes in the Eastern deanery of Nairobi. Also in Kenya, Maryknollers founded Ukweli Video, the unique Maryknoll Institute of African Studies, the Fine Arts School in Buru Buru Phase Two, and have worked in fourteen of the twenty dioceses of Kenya.

Likewise, Maryknollers branched out into apostolates in Uganda, Zambia, Ethiopia, Eritrea, Nigeria, Namibia, and Mozambique, Egypt, Somalia, South Africa, Sudan and Zimbabwe.

There are three Maryknoll priests buried in Saint Austin's cemetery in Nairobi, two in Musoma and two in Shinyanga, Tanzania. Another fifty Maryknoll Fathers and Brothers who had lived and worked in Africa passed away in the US and were buried at Maryknoll, New York.

Encountering African Spirituality

What is most interesting about the journey of Maryknollers into Africa is that we unknowingly encountered and engaged a fully formed African religious tradition and spirituality that was and is the glue that gives these societies their vitality and life. We unconsciously presented the good news of the Gospel as a heavily dogmatic theological system, with beliefs and rituals that had to be learned rather than as a light and leaven engaging the local cultural theologies. Furthermore, we were unaware that our preaching was tainted by our Westernized, secular, impersonal, objectified worldview. It was thought that Africans were devoid of any real spiritually, and we were bringing the good news of Christianity to those in the darkness of paganism – in a sense, they were a tabula rasa religiously. For example, I was given a US Baltimore Catechism that had been translated into Luo as the catechetical instrument for instructing the "readers," those preparing for baptism – an instrument that had no roots in the people's mindset or cultural traditions. Again, I was often preaching that if you didn't attend Mass on Sunday on a regular basis, you would forget about God. People were astonished at what I was saying as they couldn't imagine that their God, who surrounds and sustains them, could ever be ignored. Finally one of them commented that the only reason they could think of for this kind of preaching was that I wanted them in church on a regular basis so I could gather the collection (the Sadaka).

However, this Westernized evangelistic approach clashed with the personalized, sacral, participatory worldview of the Africans. The end game was and is a stand off, creating a kind of dual religious consciousness on the part of those converted to Christianity. However, what is not understood, appreciated, or rarely spoken about is how we, the missionaries, were in turn informally evangelized by our direct contacts with African spirituality, with its attitudes towards life and relationships, towards the environment and towards the transcendent God.

Now, after forty eight years in Africa, my Christian spiritually has been challenged, reshaped, and modified by my contacts with African spirituality to the point that I have appropriated many of its foundational beliefs, attitudes and rituals: for example, the absolute necessity to care for the elderly, the need to think about property as belonging to the whole community, and to see evil as flowing from the human heart without a need for a cosmic principle of evil. The effect is that I now realize that I have a dual religious consciousness similar to that of my African colleagues. And, I would argue that this is an inevitable result of the encounter between Christian religion and African religion, between Christian spirituality and African spirituality, between Christian theology and African theology, and not an aberration, as it is so often called. Indeed, African spirituality is so deeply embedded within African cultural identity, that if you were successful in stamping out and replacing African spirituality, then you would also stamp out and destroy African identity. And this is the reason for the resilience of African spiritually when encountering and engaging Christianity. This has resulted in the ongoing Africanization of Christianity on the one hand, and the Christianization of African spiritually on the other.

Contemporary shifts in Mission

The very idea of being evangelized by my African friends brings us to the focus of this symposium. Just as the center of Christianity has moved from the Global North to the Global South, so also has the missionary outreach which has almost disappeared in the Global North sprung up in the South, sending African missionaries into all parts of Africa with its 2000 plus cultures, and into the secularized Western world to evangelize parishes, preach the good news and maintain the vitality of the Christian communities, that is, to define and implement the mission agenda of this century. Indeed, the very vocation and calling of the Spirit that brought me into Africa as a

Christian missionary is the same vocation and calling of the Spirit of Christ that is sending Africans into all parts of the world to preach the Kerygma. It is the sign of the maturity, faith and commitment of the African Christians.

But this is not by accident; every Christian is called to preach the good news of the Christ event. So missionary activity is part and parcel of everyone's faith commitment, and it has been a feature of the newly formed Christian Churches from the beginning. For example, people in the early stages of the church in Musoma Diocese would physically move to Musoma, set up houses and farms, and study for two or three years until they were baptized. Then they would go back to their home areas as evangelists and begin to form a local church community. Indeed, in a survey in the Bunda area of the diocese some years ago, the question asked was, "Why did you choose to join the Catholic Church?" The most frequent response was that they were attracted to it and invited by their friends; little or nothing was said about Catholic doctrine, except that the teaching about the resurrection gave them a new understanding of what would happen after death. The additional element to this common missionary vocation is that now a large number of African Christians, by means of Religious Institutes and Communities, are going far and wide in spreading the gospel. The recruitment of large numbers of missionaries from India, South Korea and Africa for US dioceses, and the presence in the US of an African missionary congregation, Apostles of Jesus, all indicate the growing commitment in the Global South to mission – a commitment that is founded on the common missionary commitment of all baptized Christians.

In a fundamental sense, the Maryknoll evangelizing mission to Africa has come full circle with the African Christians responding with a missionary outreach that is second to none. In a fundamental way, this missionary activity of the African churches is the culmination of our Maryknoll vocations – the missionary torch has been successfully passed on to the African church. And it is this missionary endeavor of the African church that we are discussing, acknowledging and celebrating in this symposium. The questions raised here are the major issues and needs about which African evangelizers should be thinking as they take a more directive role in global mission, especially in the areas of evangelization among marginalized groups, interreligious dialogue, social and economic development, issues of Justice and peace and stewardship of the environment.

Conclusion

A final point is that the original thrust of Maryknoll's missionary activity into China was evangelization of the Chinese people and establishing Christian communities. These communities, as they grew, created need for routine pastoral care. As a result, they limited the time and energy needed to reach out to those not yet evangelized. This same predicament was experiences by Maryknollers in the newly developed Maryknoll dioceses of Musoma and Shinyanga.

Furthermore, by the time of my ordination in 1963, a new dimension had been added to the evangelization process, that of social and economic development. It was seen as an integral part of the process, for how could you preach God's love and forgiveness to people who were living on the margin, hungry, sick, without education and adequate shelter? So schools, small scale development project, dispensaries and hospitals were seen as integral to the evangelization process, and they spread like wild fires throughout Africa as part and parcel of missionary endeavors.

Now, within the present decade, another paradigm shift is coming to the fore, namely, the Mission to Justice. For, how can there be a thriving Christian community if one lives in fear and violence, is dispossessed of land and resources, unable to obtain justice within local tribunals, and endures the destruction of the environment on which one's human life depends? These are the topics of this afternoon's presentations which will be discussed in the breakout groups.

Again, welcome to all as we celebrate through this symposium the one hundredth anniversary of the Maryknoll missionary society.

Rev. Prof. Michael C. Kirwen, M.M., is a professor of interdisciplinary studies, and the Founder, Director, and Dean of Studies of the Maryknoll Institute of African Studies, and an Associate Dean of Saint Mary's University, MN/USA. He holds a Ph.D. in theology in the area of special interdisciplinary studies combining theology and anthropology from the University of Saint Michael's College, Toronto. As a Maryknoll missioner, he has been a resident of East Africa since 1963 combining pastoral work among the Luo people with writing, field research, and teaching.

Does the Church Have a Role in Economic Justice?

Dr. Emmanuel Manyasa

Economic justice is a phrase that is, on the face of it, fraught with contradictions. The concept of justice seems irreconcilable with the principles of rationality and self-interest upon which economics as a discipline is based. Rationality, when superficially interpreted, means exploitation of resources and circumstances for maximum returns to oneself. Among these resources is human labor, which plays a key role in production and accumulation of wealth. This connotes exploitation of unfair power distribution to one's advantage, thus creating incentive for deliberate propagation of such power imbalances. It would be imagined that the term justice is totally strange to the economic thought.

Modern economists, however, are heirs to a long tradition of thought and action on economic dimensions of social organization. Some of the thoughts are outright cold-blooded. They view human beings only in terms of their productive value. These are views that, in the past, encouraged slavery and all violations that accompanied it. In contemporary times, they regard children, the disabled and the elderly as unnecessary burdens that crowd out people's productivity and impede their enjoyment of deserved liberties through the duty of care. These are the thoughts that inform the agitation for liberal abortion laws and fuel the "mercy killing" debate – because the value of a human being is quantified in how much one is able to produce.

Prior to and after ceasing being productive, one's humanity and its sanctity don't exist.

This is a view that has deeply permeated our society. Indeed, today, it is not uncommon to meet someone for the first time, and when you introduce yourself, their first question to you is: what do you do? The question is not entirely unpleasant. It is nonetheless loathsome to the extent that it turns people into "human doings" instead of the "human beings" God intended them to be. It is more loathsome when you discern that the questioner intends to use the answer to determine whether or not you are worthy their continued engagement with. The answer, on the other hand, can be very easy to give if you are doing something specific and of which you are proud. It can be very difficult if you are doing nothing in particular or, sadly, you are one of the many victims of chronic underemployment that pervades our society.

Other economic thoughts are, however, unrealistically altruistic. Those on this side of economic thought divide envisage a world where everyone has rights and no one has obligations. All responsibility belongs to the state, which is strong and benevolent. It is an ideal world conceived by Karl Marx, where all people are assumed to be magnanimous enough to contribute to a common pool according to their ability and receive from it according to their need without cheating the system[1] – where people can live without breaking a sweat as ordered by God, because others owe them a living; where citizens of a country have rights while obligations are shouldered by the government.

Societies throughout the world have grappled with the choice between the two extreme forms of economic organization. The challenge has been and continues to be finding an optimal mix of the two, since neither is good enough by itself. In the process of choosing from the mix, some societies have emerged as left-leaning (tending towards communism) while others are right-leaning (tending towards capitalism). Experience in various countries, however, has shown that

[1] Ernest Mandel, "Marx's Theory of Surplus Value" http://www.internationalviewpoint.org/spip. php?article287. Accessed on 30.03. 2011

[2] Michael P. Todaro and Steven C. Smith, Economic Development, Eighth Edition, Fourth Indian Reprint, (Delhi: Pearson Education Ltd, 2005).

it impossible to implement any of the forms of economic organization in its pure form[2].

The Capitalist View

A pure capitalist system is rooted in classical economics where markets reign supreme and inequality is good for the economy. The market is assumed to be characterized by even distribution of power, buttressed by perfect information. Everyone acts in self-interest and every person is clever enough to obtain fair value for whatever it is they offer through the market. This way, an equilibrium outcome that leaves everyone happy is achieved. Markets are thus considered efficient and just in allocation of resources and opportunities. What is fair, though, is not necessarily equitable. The system acknowledges that, in practice, there exists asymmetry of power distribution in favor of the owners of capital over suppliers of labor, and that the asymmetry influences distribution of goods and services in the economy in favor of capital owners, thus generating inequality in welfare distribution. But inequality is considered an inevitable consequence of development[3], or, indeed, necessary for development[4] in the sense that it guarantees sustained supply of cheap labor.

With human beings seen only as inputs into the production process, it does not matter that the majority of them who are suppliers of labor languish in poverty. In fact, laborers are perceived as people who should aspire to nothing more than survival, and should thus be content earning a subsistence wage, that is, earn just enough to enable them to produce the next generation of laborers. This line of thought is still manifest in modern capitalist systems, in the form of deliberately weakened trade unions and an increasing number of the working poor. Trade unions are considered to be the vehicles through which the noisy factor of production, called labor, raises trouble for employers, thus adversely affecting production. In Kenya, this is manifest through

---

3   Simon Kuznets, "Economic Growth and Income Inequality," American Economic Review, 45 (1955): 1-28.
4   W. Arthur Lewis, "Economic Development with Unlimited Supplies of Labor," Manchester School of Economics and Social Studies, 22 (1954): 312-341.

balkanization of society, especially in cities, where millions of poor people subsist in close proximity with a few mega-rich individuals.

The Marxist View

Standing in opposition to capitalism is Marxism, which sought to eliminate the owners of capital from the economic equation and transfer their role to popular governments. Governments were seen as the legitimate custodians of public interest, thus safe to be entrusted with national resources. In this view, private firms and individual investors are evils whose only role in the economy is exploitation of the poor who supply labor. Proponents of this system of economic organization clearly ignore the reality of government failure, especially in developing countries. They also ignore the fact that real life is much more complex than populist sloganeering. In the real world, social fractionalization as well as sectarianism inhibits existence of the kind of state Marx envisaged. The struggle to control the state among these varied interest groups precludes a strong and benevolent state by ushering in subjugation and domination.

Sources of Economic Injustices in Kenya

One main source of economic injustice is absence of information about the impact of economic processes on people's wellbeing and human dignity. Developing countries generally have virtually no statistics anywhere on most of the aspects of life that really matter, such as the average distance people have to carry water and food; the numbers dying from preventable diseases; the extent of overcrowding; the prevalence of violence; or the number of people who are unable to multiply one number by another, or summarize their own country's history[5].

Naturally, there is no official data anywhere on the number of those tortured or extra judicially killed by the police, or prevalence

---

[5] Dudley Seers, The Political Economy of Nationalism (New York, Oxford University Press, 1983), PAGE.

of crime: "Many of the more important social factors are inherently unquantifiable: the chance of an objective trial, or how corruption affects policy decisions. But to say that these factors cannot be quantified – and are embarrassing subjects for those in power – does not mean that they are unimportant or can be overlooked [when assessing] a country's development."[6]

There is a conspiracy of silence about the issues that affect the poor and thus act against the poor. The poor and other vulnerable people are so unimportant that, despite their large numbers, they remain invisible, except as summarized statistics, and contentious statistics for that matter. Government officials do not even agree among themselves on official numbers of the poor. The disagreement is worse on the distribution across the country of the poor and vulnerable people[7]. Because there is no information on these issues, it means they are neither discussed nor factored into policy decisions. The poor are, in effect, crowded out of the policy table and left to endure the consequences of pro-rich policies.

Besides this conspiracy, economic injustice in our society is also rooted in lack of access to quality education. It starts with children of high aptitude missing out on the opportunity to get quality education. In Kenya, exclusion of children from poor households from quality education[8] has been entrenched through the haphazard implementation of free primary education program. In principle, the program is a pro-poor policy. However, as practiced, it is turning out to be the most powerful tool for social segregation and economic exclusion. Its proponents argue that it has managed to put more children in school, which is true. But they ignore an important question, why the public primary school teachers, who are among the low-income earners in the country, strain financially to enroll their own children in private schools. The only logical explanation is that they know first hand that there is no learning going own in public primary schools.

This denial of children from poor households of the opportunity to

---

[6]   Seers, The Political Economy.
[7]   Republic of Kenya, Economic Survey (Nairobi: Government Printer, 2007).
[8]   Raquel Fernández and Richard Rogerson, "Sorting and Long-Run Inequality," The Quarterly Journal of Economics, 116: 4 (2001), 1305-1341.

develop their God-given abilities that would yield returns to them and their families in their adult lives constitutes monumental economic injustice. It gives children of privilege, who may be of lower aptitude, the career and income opportunities that would, in a fair system with equal opportunities to education, belong to high aptitude children from disadvantaged families. Blocked from the only path to legitimate means of self-improvement, such children are condemned to a life of unemployment or underemployment at best, or to a path of self-destruction through drug abuse and crime. The consequence of this is economic segmentation into the rich and poor that overlaps with the social cleavage separating the happy from the bitter segments of society[9]. These segments henceforth live at cross-purposes.

Yet, employment determines the dignity of one's life as well as many other opportunities. One's employment situation for instance, determines which kind of friends one has and whether one has friends at all, in the true sense of the word. According to the marriage market model, it determines which kind of spouse one ends up with and the income path that the family they start follows[10]. When the number of such victims increases to the point where they form the large majority of the citizens of a country, as is the case in Kenya today, an ominous cloud hangs over the nation's future because the probability for the poor to get inextricably trapped in poverty increases through social sorting mechanisms.

Ethnic rivalry and attempts to promote separate development informs a large part of the economic injustices perpetrated by the state in Kenya. Successive governments since independence have been captured by the ethnic elite from the president's community, who invariably seek to empower themselves and their kin at the expense of other communities. The ethno-based policies of the government have failed to unite Kenyans and mobilize synergies from different segments

---

[9]   Society for International Development (2004), Pulling Apart: Facts and Figures on Inequality in Kenya (Nairobi: Society for International Development, 2004).
[10] S. Gary Becker, The Journal of Political Economy, 81:4 (1973), 813-846
[11] Emmanuel Manyasa, "Ethnic Conflicts, Social Capital and Economic Empowerment of Rural Women in Kenya." A Research Project Report for the 17th OSSREA Gender Issues Research Grant (2007). Unpublished.

of society to overcome national challenges, including the delivery of social and economic justice. In the process, they only succeed to drive the country along the path of conflict and the erosion of the poor's only asset: social capital[11].

Lack of intergenerational accountability contributes significantly to economic injustice. The current generation overindulges itself in total disregard of its obligations to the next generation. At household level, parents bring forth children and make no plans to provide for them. Some, especially fathers, even disown their children, setting them off on an extremely rocky path of life that is fraught with many risks. Many other parents live as though they don't have children in the first place. The consequence is children ending up in child labor to eke out a living at best, or, at worst, they are trafficked and inducted into social ills like prostitution and crime.

It is not uncommon to find a man who has consumed what was produced by three generations in his lifetime. A man inherits property from his parents (usually land) and sells to consume. He is employed for many years, works and earns a decent income, which he consumes entirely. During his retirement years, he depends on his children, whom he may have refused to educate in the first place, to support him. This constitutes enormous economic injustice, which incidentally is neither noticed nor discussed at policy level.

At society level, lack of intergenerational accountability explains the overexploitation of natural resources. Riparian lands and water catchment areas have been cleared and converted into farmlands that cause siltation and drying up of rivers, without regards to future generations' needs. Short-term profiteering reigns supreme in all matters of resources allocation and utilization. The state on the other hand, continues to borrow and spend the money on non-priority projects for short-term political expediency, in total disregard of the heavy penalties the debt imposes on future generations.

Besides lack of intergenerational accountability, being embedded in a poor family and/or neighborhood exerts social taxation on individuals'

---

[12] Abhijit Banerjee and Esther Duflo, "Growth Theory through the Lens of Development Economics," http://econ-www.mit.edu/faculty (2004). Accessed on 12.06.2007.

resources. This compounds the effects of credit constraints. It is argued that specific claims by members of the household, extended family, or neighbors on one's income stream may convert rational individuals into "hyperbolic discounters"[12] This enhances lack of intergenerational accountability and creates economic agents that neither act within the rationality principle nor with Christian generosity.

Corruption is perhaps the most important source of economic injustice in Kenya. It has permeated all sectors of the economy, with deadly effect on poor people. For instance, it pushes income opportunities beyond the reach of forthright, politically neutral individuals and firms. Thus it enriches the wicked and incompetent while crowding out from the economy the forthright players whose initiatives would otherwise impact positively the lives of many other citizens. Thanks to corruption, public tenders are won by those with neither capacity nor intention to deliver public goods and services. Through corruption, public resources are transferred to private individuals, thus excluding the majority of the people from their use. This doubly hurts the poor who must rely on run-down public facilities because they cannot afford the overpriced private ones, yet still pay unaffordable rates to shoulder the burden of corruption.

Corruption also underlies the widespread practice of unfair and illegal employment practices. There are laws that govern employer-employee relations, but they are never enforced due to collusion between unscrupulous employers and Ministry of Labor officials. Minimum wage legislation is one of the most abused pieces of legislation in the country, with many labor officers preferring to take bribes from employers rather than enforce the law for the benefit of the low income workers. The consequence of corruption in the labor market is an increasing numbers of the working poor.

---

[13] Adam Smith, An Inquiry into the Nature and Causes of the Wealth of Nations (1776). http://www. econlib.org/library/Smith/smMS.html. Accessed on 15.05.2007.

The Quest for Economic Justice

The quest for economic justice can be traced back to Adam Smith. Smith, widely considered the father of development economics, posed the million ton, perennial question: Why are all societies not equally prosperous?[13]. This could be rephrased: Why are all people not equally prosperous? Why do some people live in obscene levels of comfort while many others languish in extreme and dehumanizing poverty? Smith's question stimulated research seeking to understand disparities in levels of economic prosperity among nations, particularly between North America and Western Europe on the one hand, and the rest of the world on the other. The resultant literature sought to explain the disparities and also to provide a roadmap for the less developed countries to uplift themselves. The focus was on aggregate measures of national prosperity (gross national product GNP), with little regard to its distribution.

In 1969, Dudley Seers signaled the shift away from the goal of growth by posing the following questions about a country's development: "What has been happening to poverty? What has been happening to unemployment? What has been happening to inequality? If all three of these have become less severe, then beyond doubt this has been a period of development for the country concerned. If one or two of these central problems have been growing worse, especially if all three have, it would be strange to call the result 'development', even if per capita income has soared."[14]

Amartya Sen concurs, arguing that development involves reducing deprivation and broadening choice. He asserts that freedom – not development – is the ultimate goal of economic life as well as the most efficient means of realizing general welfare. Overcoming deprivations is central to development. Unfreedoms include hunger, famine, ignorance, an unsustainable economic life, unemployment, barriers to economic fulfillment by women or minority communities, premature

---

[14] Dudley Seers, "The Meaning of Development," International Development Review, 11 (1969): 3-4.
[15] Amartya Sen, Development as Freedom (New York: Oxford University Press, 1999) PAGE????.
[16] D. Jeffrey Sachs, The End of Poverty: Economic Possibilities of Our Time (New York: Penguin Press, 2005), PAGE???.

death, political persecution, threats to the environment, and luck of access to health, sanitation, or clean water. Freedom of exchange, labor contract, social opportunities, and protective security are not just ends or constituent components of development but also important means to development and freedom.[15]

Jeffrey D. Sachs believes that the world has enough resources to rid every human being, especially those in the developing countries, of the indignity of poverty and malnutrition[16]. He calls for commitment by developed countries to devote resources to provision of healthcare, good nutrition, and education, to end poverty among the most vulnerable populations of the world. Once the cycle of poverty is broken, the poor would be able to sustainably improve their lot without further support.

The Role of the Church in Economic Justice

To begin with, the church underscores the fact that basic justice demands that people be assured of a minimum level of participation in the economy. "Every perspective on economic life that is human, moral and Christian must be shaped by three questions: What does the economy do for people? What does it do to people? And how do people participate in it?"[17] In the 1986 Pastoral Letter, the U.S. Catholic Bishops exhorted the faithful to judge the economy "not by what it produces but also by how it touches human life and whether it protects or undermines the dignity of the human person."[18]

According to Pope John Paul II, workers, owners, managers, stockholders and consumers are moral agents in economic life. By their choices, initiative, creativity and investment, they either enhance or diminish economic opportunity, community life and social justice. Inherent in this argument is the fact that individuals have the responsibility to ensure that the systems they put in place for purposes of production and distribution of goods and services guarantee equitable

---

[17] U.S. Catholic Bishops, "Pastoral Letter on Catholic Social Teaching and the U.S. Economy (1986), no. 7. http://www.osjspm.org/majordoc_us_bishops_statements_economic_justice_for_all.aspx

[18] U.S. Catholic Bishops, no. 4.

access to the economy. Economic justice is achievable only when such systems that are products of deliberate human design provide decent livelihood opportunities for all in the society. As Pope John XXIII declared, "all people have a right to life, food, clothing, shelter, rest, medical care, education, and employment." Provision of these necessities to all people would make the world a just place.

But this is not the case in any country in the world, and it is far from being the case in Kenya. This means that the work of all those who wish to contribute to economic justice is cut out for them. But first, it is necessary to understand why personal initiatives as envisaged by Pope John XXIII have either not been undertaken, or have been undertaken in measures that are inadequate to deliver the desired transformation. The answer may lie in the words of Elizabeth Wordsworth, who, in her poem "Clever and Good," argues that "If all the good people were clever and all clever people were good, the world would be nicer than ever we thought that it possibly could."[20]

From Wordsworth's words, it can be concluded that there are far too many bad clever people and too many good people who aren't clever. Indeed Wordsworth further argues that "The good are so harsh to the clever; the clever so rude to the good!"[21] This is the challenge that faces the church and mission: to create a critical mass of good clever people through both conversion of clever bad people and intellectual formation of new good ones, but also to mediate between the two groups and ensure that fruitful dialogue happens that narrows the gap between their positions on important economic justice matters.

In Kenya, the church has done well in creating a critical mass of good clever people through provision of intellectual and spiritual formation opportunities for intelligent young Kenyans. The church has not done well in mediating between the arrogant, clever bad people and the judgmental good people. Often the church has found itself, rightfully, on the same side with the judgmental good people, thereby vitiating its ability to command the arrogant clever ones. This can be

---

[20] Wordsworth, Elizabeth (1986), Clever and Good, http://www.poems.net.au/clever-and-good-elizabeth-wordsworth. Accessed on 31.03.2011.
[21] Wordsworth, "The Clever."

changed to foster consensus-building that will pave the way for just policies and managerial systems to be instituted.

The American Bishops in their Pastoral Letter provide markers that should be used to evaluate the economy. The church thus has an obligation, as the custodian of moral values, to frequently conduct audits of government and corporate policies with regards to employment, political and economic freedoms, and issue communiqués that will serve as the moral compass for other economic players. This, if done consistently and in a structured form, may challenge the bad people intellectually and compel them to listen to the views of the good people who may not be as intellectually deep. Besides, this will help end the conspiracy of silence against the poor and push their issues on to the policy table.

The church is itself a reservoir of intellectual power. This can be harnessed to mount a structured, peaceful, assault on largely outdated economic, business and political philosophies and practices that violate human dignity. But this would require some ideological shift within the church, from the more conservative view that regards salvation of human souls as the only mandate of its mission to a more progressive approach that seeks to promote human welfare in all its forms.

Finally, the church has great capacity to mobilize resources. Without creating dependency, the church can design economic programs to support vulnerable groups in the initial stages in their self economic empowerment efforts. This can be through provision of seed money to start businesses or setting up group projects and gradually handing them over to the communities to manage. This the church in Kenya has done quite well, especially in marginal areas of the country. But it can be improved and up-scaled, utilizing the experience gained over the many years that this has been going on.

Dr. Emmanuel Manyasa is a senior lecturer in the school of Economics, Kenyatta University, Nairobi, Kenya. He holds a Ph.D. in Economics and MA in Economics both from Kenyatta University. He is a prolific researcher with OSSREA and has won several grants for research.

Break-out Discussion Group Report on Economic Justice

Mr. Francis Kimani

• Un-uniform access to education is an injustice. All children should have an equal right to education.

• Being denied access to quality education hinders one to access optimal education and hence exploit one's potential to the optimum.

• Inculcation of morality and responsibility is crucial in ensuring that people don't do injustice to others.

• Empowering of day schools through policy making to ensure equal and affordable access to education is necessary.

• Christians must be among those who initiate the idea of change, speak out against injustice, and work towards changing unjust policies through, for example, using Christians in positions of power.

• There is need for research to show that although there is economic growth, we still have many people becoming poorer and poorer.

• There is need to re-think the kind of education that children should be given in order to make positive contributions in the economy.

• How do we package our education so that it can inculcate moral values in the society?

- There is need for more involvement of institutions of higher learning in development of policies, e.g. Vision 2030.

- There has to be proper investment and emphasis on higher education so as to provide the required human capital to drive the economy.

- The provision of education is highly commercialized, hence providing only holders of certificates who are intellectually incapable.

- There is need to impact moral values in children at home and avoid children spending all their time in school, i.e., from kindergarten at age two to University.

- Improving the teachers pay alone can't change the quality of education; the inculcation of ethics is more important.

- Donor funds are making people too dependent on the donations, leading to reduced self-worth and dependence syndrome. Intervention during times of crisis should be strategized to feature the time duration and post intervention strategies.

- There is need to eliminate the "job color" mentality.

- We have to eradicate corruption.

- We have to change the government's taxing policies: increased taxes scare off investors or make them cut down on employment or the workers' wages.

Mr. Francis Kimani is a graduate in finance from Kenyatta University and a CPA. He is currently working as a finance officer for Maryknoll Fathers and Brothers, Africa Region.

Discovering the Role of the Church in the Protection of Civilians in Peace Support Operations

Dr. C.A. Mumma-Martinon

This paper looks at the Catholic Church and its role in the protection of civilians during armed conflicts. The introduction gives the realities and impacts of armed conflict on civilians and describes who the civilians are. The second section examines some of the issues surrounding civilians which call for protection and what efforts are being made by the international community to do so. The third section introduces the church and examines its important role in this scenario, where there are many stakeholders and each has to play its role very distinctively towards an effective protection of civilians. Suggestions are made of areas and how the church contributes to protection of civilians with references to specific categories.

Background to the Protection of Civilians

Kofi Annan, the former UN Secretary General stated that,

As human beings, we cannot be neutral, or at least have no right to be, when other human beings are suffering. Each of us must do what he or she can to help those in need, even though it would be much safer and more comfortable to do nothing.

In the past fifty years, our world has been ravaged by violent conflicts that have claimed the lives of many millions of civilians and left tens of millions more permanently displaced. These civilians have been expelled from their homes, and are often denied access to life-saving food, medicine and shelter. Grave violations of international humanitarian and human rights law and blatant disrespect for the normative framework of humanity that has emerged over the past 50 years is common to many of these conflicts. Civilians have become the primary target of attack motivated by ethnic or religious hatred, political confrontation or simply ruthless pursuit of economic interests.

This stark picture has led the United Nations, the International Committee of the Red Cross, regional organizations and many other international agencies increasingly to dedicate greater attention to protecting civilians in ongoing armed conflicts. The United Nations Secretary-General,Kofi Annan, called for the establishment of a "culture of protection" in his report of 30 March 2001 on the Protection of Civilians in Armed Conflict. In such a culture, Governments would live up to their responsibilities, armed groups would respect the recognized rules of international humanitarian law, the private sector would be conscious of the impact of its engagement in crisis areas, and Member States and international organizations would display the necessary commitment to ensure decisive and rapid action in the face of crisis. And it is in this culture that the church has to find its place towards achieving the same objective. The establishment of this culture will depend on the willingness of Member States not only to adopt some of the measures, but also to deal with the reality of armed groups and other non-state actors in conflicts, and the role of civil society in moving from vulnerability to security and from war to peace. Historically, wars have been fought between states in accordance with the rules of war outlined in the Geneva Conventions. In those conventional wars casualties were among combatants rather than civilians. In contrast, today's wars are more likely to be within states where civilians, not combatants, sustain the most casualties.

It should be noted that when armed conflicts breakout civilians usually find themselves as refugees or Internally Displaced persons (IDPs).[1] This has been the case in many African countries (e.g. Rwanda, Burundi, Uganda, Sudan, and Congo, just to mention a few).

---

[1] The IDPs usually comprise mainly of women with their children and the elderly men. The young men are usually out fighting or with rebel groups (UNAMID Joint Mission Analysis, 2011).

Problem Statement

Ensuring the safety and security of civilians during armed conflicts is becoming more and more critical in peace support operations. So long as the security of civilians is not addressed, a viable peace cannot be achieved. In the midst of conflict, there are hundreds of thousands of civilians — women, men and children — who are confronted with the horrors, pain and suffering of war on a daily basis. Whether as the intended targets of attack or the incidental victims of the use of force, civilians continue to account for the majority of casualties in conflict. Thus, the protection of civilians has become the very essence of peacekeeping. The 1999 UN Report (S/2010/579) emphasizes the fundamental need to focus efforts on making a tangible difference in situations where protection of civilians is needed most. For a decade, the UN Security Council has also expressed its resolve to support more effective missions, and to put greater spotlight on the protection of civilians, as seen by its series of statements and resolutions, and the request that the Secretary General issue regular reports on the protection of civilians in armed conflicts.[2]

Protection of Civilians in the Context of Peace Support Operations

In this paper, civilians refer to the principal victims who are normally from poor families and vulnerable groups, like women, children, persons with disabilities and the elderly. These groups cannot flee easily and are at greater risk of death and injury.

Modern peacekeeping missions are multidimensional in nature, addressing the full spectrum of peace building activities, from

---

[2] The United Nations Security Council (UNSC) resolutions on the protection of civilians include: S/RES/1267 of October 1999, S/RES/1296 of 19th April 2000, S/RES/1674 of April 28 2006, and S/RES/ of 23 December 2006. The President of the Security Council has issued statements on the protection of civilians on 12 February 1999 (S/PRST/1999/6); 15 March, 2002 (S/PRST/2002/20); December 2002 (S/PRST/2002/41); 15 December 2003 (S/PRST/2003/27); 14 December 2004(S/PRST2004/46); 21 June 2005 (S/PRST2005/25) and 14 January 2009 ((S/PRST/2009/1). The Secretary General has submitted periodic reports on the protection of civilians, on 8 September 1999, (S/1999/957); 31 March 2001 (S/201/331); 26 2002 (S/2002/1300), 28 May 2004 (S/2004/431); 28 November 2005 (S/2005/740); 28 October 2007 (S/2007/643) and 29 May 2009/277).

providing secure environments to monitoring human rights and rebuilding the capacity of the state. Increasingly, such mandates also instruct peacekeeping missions to put an emphasis on the physical protection of civilians.

Protection of civilians (POC), fundamentally, as both a broad concept and specifically within the context of peacekeeping, remains open to a number of interpretations. Protection could refer to all activities aimed at obtaining full respect for the rights of the individual in accordance with the letter and spirit of relevant bodies of law (i.e. human rights law, international humanitarian law and refugee's law) or would involve a wide range process with distinctive responsibilities for each stakeholder /protection/ actor.

It should be noted that during armed conflicts, the people to be protected are usually numerically more than the protectors and the mission staff themselves. The area of operation for any mission is usually huge and cannot be covered by the mission staff alone, or adequately. This is the case of Darfur in Sudan. The reality is that the protectors, especially the mission staff, cannot cover and protect everyone. The Church could thus make a contribution, in working with and supporting the mission staff and other protectors in various peace building activities, both within the IDP/refugee camps and among the population.

The Changing Role of the Church in Protection of Civilians in Armed Conflict

Whether viewed in terms of physical or legal safety, the protection of civilians is the primary responsibility of national governments, given their sovereign responsibility for, and authority over, all those living within their territory. It is only when protection by national governments is inadequate, due either to a lack of willingness or capacity, that external actors from the local and international community may have a responsibility to protect civilians in their respective countries and areas of jurisdictions.

The Church plays an important protective role which includes responsive action which aims to prevent or halt a specific pattern of abuse or alleviate its immediate effects; remedial action, which takes place after abuse, and aims to restore people's dignity and ensure adequate living conditions through reparation, restitution and rehabilitation; and, finally, environment-building, which aims to foster an environment conducive to respect for the rights of individuals in accordance with the relevant bodies of law.[3] These activities are to be taken forward parallel with other actors (political, military, police and other civilian components, including human rights groups, children protectors, and gender units, just to mention a few), as part of what is considered to be a collective obligation to protect civilians when the responsible actors fail to do so.

Despite the fact that the church has done a lot towards peace building activities all over the world during conflict situations,[4] the role of the church in protecting civilians during armed conflicts and with specific reference to missions[5] has not been highlighted or studied extensively. The authors of references concerning the issue have limited themselves to marginal comments about the church in its protection role. Church scholars, on the other hand, have produced a substantial amount of literature on the church, but they focus mainly on church and politics[6] and not on issues that pertain specifically to protection of civilians within the context of Peace Support Operations.

In the post-Vatican II era, the church significantly became involved in the political and social struggles of different countries; it became the "voice of those without a voice" and a primary defender of human rights, where many recommended a prophetic option for the poor. Church involvement in politics varied from country to country, but in

---

[3] Giossi Caverzasio, *Strengthening Protection in War: A Search for Professional Standards*, (Geneva: 2001), 21.

[4] During the 1994 genocide in Rwanda, Bishop Abbot Baudouin Busunyu (Nkanka Parish, Kamembe, Cyangugu) was a shining example of bravery despite opposition from his elder parish priest and his entire family. He discreetly organized his refugee's flight to eastern DR Congo, and even escorted the refugees to the border. Also, Abbot Jean Pierre Ngoga of Kibeho Parish, Gikongoro Province, received over 30,000 IDPs at his parish, though he was unable to save their lives.

[5] Missions here refer to multidimensional, contemporary Peace Support Operations, comprising the military, the police and civilians. Examples here could include: UNMID and UNMIS in Sudan, MONUSCO in Congo, UNMIL, etc.

[6] Emelio Betances, "The Catholic Church and Political Mediation in the Dominican Republic: a Comparative Perspective." Journal of Church and State, 46 (2004): 341-350.

general one notes the emergence of a commitment among the clergy to seek social justice. With the changing nature of conflict in Africa, it has become evident that the church needs to be more proactively involved in all situations of conflict.

The advantage the church has as opposed to governments or other political entities is that it can play a very important role in protecting civilians as an impartial entity because the Church neither has nor abrogates a "political formula," but it does have criteria and principles according to which lay Christians could create feasible and correct political formulas. The church has the opportunity to offer a framework of a plurality of possible systems, regimes, models and projects, which are open to lawful and careful human action to face the great challenges of protecting civilians in armed conflicts. The church can also maintain itself free from all affiliations, if it decides to do so, to protect civilians. It is in a position to avoid all opportunistic reasons for not protecting civilians, but instead respect the autonomy of temporal realities, freedom, and the rights of civilians.

Specific areas of contribution by the church

Protecting Children

In the context of armed conflict, children increasingly are victims of, witnesses to, and often perpetrators of violence. They are targeted, along with other civilians, by members of warring factions in the context of armed conflict[7] to become child soldiers if boys and /or wives of military commanders, if girls. Forced recruitment, often with police complicity, from schools, city streets and playgrounds is how children in war zones are conscripted.

According to testimony from children who have escaped, members of the Lord's Resistance Army (LRA) cross into Uganda from Sudan in small bands to loot villages, kill, maim and torture civilians, and to abduct children. They subsequently meet up with other small bands with identical agendas and march back to their rebel camps in Sudan.

---

[7] The Office of the Special Representative of the UN Secretary General for Children in Armed Conflict estimates that there are 300,000 children worldwide who have been armed with light weapons to fight on behalf of the adults who have kidnapped or conscripted them. This was the case of Northern Uganda and Sierra Leone.

Children are killed when they are unable to keep up, fail to follow instructions, or attempt to escape. New recruits are forced to participate in these summary killings in order to bind them to the exercise.

In every situation of armed conflict children in affected populations become separated from their parents or their primary caregivers. Often separation occurs during flights. At other times, families are killed and children are the lone survivors. Conversely, separation could occur if a child was not at home at the time the family was required to flee.

A lot of effort has been made to support issues related to children. Substantive conferences have been held and significant activities undertaken including the Coalition to Stop the Use of Child Soldiers.[8] The coalition in its effort to effect a global ban on child soldiers reports that the Convention on the Rights of the Child has been almost universally ratified and that the Optional Protocol to the Convention on the Rights of the Child on the Involvement of Children in Armed Conflict to raise the minimum age for direct participation in hostilities from 15 to 18 has been signed by 80 countries, ratified by five, and was expected to be in force by the end of 2001.

Demobilized Child Soldiers [9]

In this regard, the church can make a number of contributions towards the protection of civilians, including the reunification of children in cases where children have been separated from their families,[10] and identifying and placing them in foster families until

---

[8] This is an international coalition of NGOs linked to national campaigns focused on ending the use of child soldiers in rebel and government armies. In an editorial, "When Children Go to War," The *New York Times*, in its 18 June, 2001 edition, took note of the Coalition's report on the use of child soldiers by county, released on 12 June 2001. The editorial commended the comprehensiveness of the report and ended on a somber note: "But greater resources are needed to provide treatment to heal the damage done to these children of war."

[9] In cases where child soldiers have been demobilized, Olara Otunnu, the Secretary General's Special Representative for Children and Armed Conflict and Carol Bellamy, the Executive Director of UNICEF, on separate occasions, in their official capacity, visited Sierra Leone and Sudan where they spoke directly with rebel leaders and government officials about releasing soldiers of under 18 from the military.

[10] This is central to resolving the problem of separated children and family and constitutes a significant component of the efforts of local and international agencies towards this goal.

their biological families are located.[11] In part, this is because the African has a tradition of incorporating needy or abandoned children into other households.[12] The church could also work closely with the United Nations High Commissioner for Refugees (UNHCR) who is responsible for identifying separated children, monitoring their care, intervening if they are being abused or their needs are not being met, and tracing their families for eventual reunification, " make follow ups to ensure these children go to school and that adequate food is provided for them, especially in cases where the foster families are not able to do that and, in cases of abduction of children, continue condemning and forming more advocacy groups to fight for the rights of these children.

The church can also work closely with the International Red Cross that normally has reunification programs to make sure the refugees return to their homes. This was the case in Liberia and Guinea, where a program has been established through Child Protection Committees, with representation from national and local authorities, women's and teachers' associations, religious communities, refugee groups, and local NGOs.

The church can play a very important role in modifying the impact of forced migration. Child soldiers face many hardships once they return to their communities; families and community members look upon them with suspicion because of real or alleged violent acts they have committed. Often, these children are rejected upon their return. In terms of resettlement, the children face a host of problems, ranging from an unfamiliar host country and linguistic difficulty to finding appropriate educational and vocational opportunities. They thus require trained resettlement caseworkers who understand the context from which they escaped or left, and tailored assistance and programming appropriate to their situations.

---

[11]   This, according to observers, "despite the potential for neglect, abuse, or exploitation of separated children by caregivers, is generally in the best interests of the children to remain in family care settings

[12]   If done properly, fostering is both culturally relevant and in keeping with international standards for child protection. But care should be taken and the church should monitor the situation closely so that the foster families do not exploit the children and make them domestic workers.

Protecting the Youth

Within the IDP and refugees camps, there are youths who linger around and do not know what to do and ultimately join the rebel groups or armed forces as the only means of survival. This is the case in Zam Zam, the main camp in El Fasher, North Darfur, where many youths remain idle with no work opportunities and there is compulsory recruitment of the youths to join some of the armed groups, which compels many of them to flee.

Increasingly, there are circumstances where children, often adolescents, are required to take on domestic responsibility in households where parents are absent. Large-scale examples have occurred in Rwanda as a consequence of genocide and in countries where AIDS has orphaned large numbers of children. But in any case, the situation of households headed by children is one in which older children, both boys and girls, take responsibility for younger siblings and rarely with adequate resources. In such circumstances, boys have greater access to jobs, while girls are vulnerable to sexual exploitation. In all cases, adolescents who have assumed the responsibility of raising younger brothers and sisters put their own lives on hold to do so.

Providing food, shelter, clothing and, when possible, school fees and access to healthcare with scarce resources would be the greatest contribution of the church in such circumstances. For without access to land, shelter is difficult; without agricultural skills, self-sufficiency in farming will not occur; and without access to schooling, preparation for the future is bleak. The church can also start educational programs and vocational training centres, with other creative exercises to keep the youth engaged during a difficult time of displacement and disorientation. These activities can divert them from joining militias to become child soldiers as well as assist in their eventual reintegration into society.

The unfortunate reality is that education, where it exists, is for primary school children, vocational and skills training are often for women who have become single heads of household as a result of war, as is reproductive health information, AIDS awareness and access to income-generating activities. Youths, especially males, are targeted for conscription into either government or rebel militias, and females are vulnerable to sexual exploitation. In cases where there is continued neglect to the special needs of this category of civilians, the church should fill in the gap and draw on the experiences of other country programs that involve adolescents in youth leadership groups to take up campaigns on such issues as drug use, AIDS, and early marriage.[13]

Protecting the Women

"War has always dealt cruelly with women, but the nature of violent conflict in the world has changed in the past decades in ways that are taking an even greater toll on women and children."[14] In the 14 years after the end of the Cold War, from 1990 to 2003, there were 59 different major armed conflicts in 48 locations. Only four of these involved war between nations.[15] This means that fighting is now more often taking place, not on the battleground, but in the places where people live. It means that civilians are more likely to be direct or indirect targets of violence.

During such conflicts, whether during escapes and within IDPs or refugee camps, women and girls are extremely vulnerable to violence, sexual abuse and exploitation. As community structures crumble and violence escalates, there are fewer measures in place to ensure their safety and security.[16] One of the most disturbing phenomena of the past two decades is the use of rape as a deliberate tactic of war, a way of demoralizing and humiliating the enemy and destabilizing entire communities. In situations of armed conflict, girls and women are routinely targeted in campaigns of gender-based violence, including rape, mutilation, prostitution, and sexual slavery. For example, Congo is considered one of today's worst humanitarian crises, where militias have routinely engaged in rape of young girls and women of all ages, and conflict has forced more than a million people to leave their homes and seek refuge in makeshift camps for displaced persons.[17] This is

---

[13] See UNHCR 1999 Global Appeal.

[14] Bellamy, *Women in Armed Conflict at Extreme Risk of Sexual Violence*, (New York/Geneva, 25, November, 2004)

[15] Ibid.

[16] Ibid.

[17] Ibid.

made worse by the fact that women and girls are even in greater danger of being sexually assaulted, particularly when they venture beyond the camp for firewood collection or to work in their farms.[18]

To begin with, perpetrators of sexual violence during armed conflict, as well as those who authorize attacks, must be prosecuted. Doing this successfully requires concerted action of the local, national, regional, and international levels. The church can also join this effort by providing necessary support to women and girls who have endured rape and other forms of sexual violence so that they can rebuild their lives; helping with developing of security measures around IDP and refugee camps to improve security; educating women on how to protect themselves during such cases; providing guidance and counseling sessions to the victims; and providing material support in terms of food, medicine and even shelter.

Protecting Older Persons

Older persons, just like children, youth and women in armed conflict situations are also exposed to grave danger of violation of their rights and violence against them. In addition, they have vulnerabilities and needs associated with ageing that place them at particular risk. However, their special situation has been insufficiently recognized and addressed by humanitarian interventions targeted on vulnerable groups generally. Moreover, lack of understanding, even prejudice, towards older women and men often results in devaluation of their unique capacities and contributions and of the role they can and do play in the care of dependents, the mitigation of emergencies, and the recovery of war-torn societies.

The issue with the ageing of the population worldwide is that an increasing number of older persons have become victims of armed conflicts and their plight is posing new challenges for international organizations. For example, UNHCR estimates that 10% of refugees are over age 60.[19] Regrettably, the lack of attention given so far to older persons means that comprehensive information on the impact on older persons is lacking for most conflicts. Older persons like any

---

[18] Ibid.

[19] see UNHCR 1999 Global Appeal.

other persons or general population are entitled to equal protection under international human rights and humanitarian law.

Recent field research[20] has identified the following areas in which older persons face particular problems and where action by the international community is required:

Denial and Lack of Access to Humanitarian Resources

Older people "fight a losing battle in the competition for resources." Because of their poor mobility and lower physical strength, they are less able to access centralized relief and service delivery points, or to compete with others for food and medical services in chaotic emergency situations. They are often left out of emergency rationing processes.

Loss of Livelihood

Older persons are particularly at risk from the disappearance of sources of income during conflict, whether from loss of land, employment or social security/pension schemes, which impacts negatively not only on them but also on household members dependent on them. Documentation is also often lost which makes it very difficult to access assets, such as property, and benefits.

Isolation

During armed conflict, older people may be deliberately left behind to guard land and property, and also abandoned in the chaos as other family members escape. They may be unable to fend for themselves because of the destruction of communities and social support systems. Few agencies provide tracing and family reunification programs for older adults, resulting in their permanent abandonment and neglect.

Age and Gender Discrimination

The traditional skills, experience, local knowledge and coping strategies of older persons are important to mitigating the impact of conflict and to move toward social recovery. Yet their contribution

---

[20]   This information is drawn from the following studies: UNHCR Assistance to Older Refugees (1998), and Women, Children and Older Refugees: The Sex and Age Distribution of Refugee Populations with a Special Emphasis on UNHCR Policy Priorities (2001); Help Age International/ECHO/UNHCR, Older People in Disasters and Humanitarian Crises: Guidelines for Best Practice (London, 2000)

is often unrecognized and undervalued. Older persons are often seen as unproductive, unable to learn, and a "poor investment," and are therefore usually excluded from rehabilitation programs, particularly micro-credit and skills training. They are rarely, if ever, consulted in decisions affecting them, their families and communities. Emergency delivery and shelter arrangements may be incompatible with the cultural norms and beliefs of older people, leading de facto to their exclusion from emergency responses. Older women are particularly at risk in some cultures where they may be denied inheritance rights or employment opportunities even though they may have primary responsibility for the care of children and other relatives. Older persons of both genders are thus prevented from re-establishing self-sufficiency and playing a role in rebuilding their society.

In recent years, the international community has begun to take action to redress this neglect. In 2001 the UN High Commissioner for Refugees adopted a policy on older persons and, in 2002, the Second World Assembly on Ageing adopted specific policy commitments concerning older persons in emergency situations. Nevertheless, much still needs to be done both in terms of making older persons "visible" and in ensuring that their specific needs for protection and assistance are met. The Security Council can play an important role in mainstreaming concern for, and action on, older persons in its ongoing consideration of issues relating to the protection of civilians in armed conflict.

In this regard, monitoring and reporting on the situation of older persons would be the first step forward. The church, in collaboration with other stakeholders, can take action to ensure that the specific rights and needs of older persons for assistance and protection are addressed. Special measures should be taken to protect older persons in emergencies: locate and identify older persons at risk, with particular attention to the problems faced by women; ensure equal access to food, shelter, medical care and other services; facilitate evacuations and family reunification; raise awareness of older persons' needs among relief personnel. The church could ensure, through advocacy programs, that there should be increased consultation and participation of older persons in rehabilitation programs, including access to micro-credit, skills training and employment opportunities, taking into account the special problems and needs of older women. Since many people ignore the older persons in conflict situations, the church can support and take recognition of the potential of older persons as leaders in the family and community for social recovery and conflict resolution, including those living outside the country, to contribute resources to reconstruction.

Protecting Persons with Disabilities

During armed conflicts, many civilians have found themselves with disabilities due to different reasons, including injuries caused by landmines, leading to permanent impairment, disabilities, and handicaps. Landmine-caused impairment affects entire body systems and are often the most obvious and measurable characteristics of conflict. These impairments include: amputation, spinal cord injury, blindness, and burns. Landmine-caused disabilities, on the other hand consist of capacities that are normal for a person of a particular age and development. They include problems in self-care, ability to walk to school, or to perform other duties. Landmine-caused handicaps are the deficiencies of a society in accommodating to people with disabilities, including problems in earning a living, physical accessibility, social stigma and isolation.

The problem of large numbers of disabled ex-combatants, who are generally young men, must also be addressed since such abilities represent an on-going reminder of conflict to their communities and thus a source of friction.

The church, in collaboration with others, should create a situation that allows each disabled person to live a fulfilling life of self acceptance through guidance and counseling, to be self- reliant, and live a whole life in close relation with other people. It can also encourage and help families, neighbours, school children, members of the community, and others to accept, respect, feel comfortable with, assist, welcome into their lives, provide equal opportunities for, and appreciate the abilities and possibilities of disabled people. Persons with disabilities should also be encouraged to become leaders and workers in rehabilitation activities. This is one way of providing meaningful work and training for them.

More efforts should be made towards de-stigmatising persons with disabilities through promoting particular disabled persons as positive role models. In areas of conflict such as Afghanistan and Sri Lanka, community-based rehabilitation facilitates school integration of disabled refugee children and support alternatives to institutions for disabled, displaced, and orphaned children have been established. In Palestine, health and social development program personnel are educated and encouraged to avoid preferential treatment of persons injured in the Intifada. This helps to reduce inequities between injured combatants and civilians and has led to gains for all persons with disabilities which previously had been difficult to achieve.[21]

Demobilisation and re-integration support programmes (including assistive devices, referrals, home activities of daily living training, social and peer support, vocational training, income generation, leadership development) are vital to defuse tensions and demonstrate society's ongoing respect for injured veterans.

The church can also offer physical assistance to the physically disabled persons. This kind of assistance would include giving food, transportation to medical facilities for treatment, moral support, psychological assistance, and encouragement to participate in the development and implementation of various social projects and initiatives in co-operation with different local youth organizations and charities. Physically disabled persons should be encouraged to participate in cultural entertainment activities to help them overcome the impact of disability and lead a normal life.

---

[21]   W. Boyce and S. Weera, "Issues of Disability Assessment in War zones," in *Disability in Different Cultures - Reflections on Local Concepts*, ed. B.Holzer, A. Vreede and G. Weigt (Bielefeld: Transcript-verlag, 1999).

Conclusion

From the above discussion, it is evident that the active involvement of the church in the protection of civilians during armed conflicts and working with peace support operations provides the framework for the Catholic Church to participate directly in protecting civilians. It also creates the circumstances for the church to work directly with peace support operations. The advantage of the church that this paper seeks to portray is the church as a non-partisan actor in the protection of civilians. This position gives the church credibility and legitimacy in the eyes of the citizens who need protection. However, a non-partisan position does not mean neutrality, because the church is not neutral and should be proactive in condemning any violation of human rights during armed conflicts. In fact, through its non-partisan role the church defends the protection of civilians as a worthwhile cause that should be supported by all. Thus, the church can be a very special protector of civilians.

Being non-partisan can also offer the church the ability to participate in social, economic and political activities of the country of conflict, thus leading to peace building and development activities. This kind of role can allow the church to successfully dialogue and mediate with the different actors, including government authorities, the armed forces, the population, and any other stakeholder in the conflict. It is this kind of dialogue and mediation that can promote peace and reconciliation. Mediation is one tool the church can use in conflict situations because it can produce important gains that in turn improve the life of many people and could contribute significantly to political stability in any situation of conflict.

Dr. C.A. Mumma Martinon holds a Ph.D in International Conflict Management from the University of Leipzing, Germany. She has taught in many Institutions of higher learning such as Institute of Peace Studies and International Relations, Hekima College, Nairobi, Kenya, Institute of Diplomacy and International Studies, University of Nairobi, Defense Staff College and National Defense College, Karen, Nairobi. She is a distinguished consultant and conflict prevention analyst.

Break-out Group Discussion on Peace Building

Rev. John Conway, MM

The Catholic Church has a rich tradition and a library of lives and books on peace building.

- The Catholic Church is a "specialist on humanity."
- The Catholic Church should not present itself as either military or police. It is extremely important to avoid any confusion of roles.
- The Catholic Church is to be organically involved in conflict prevention, conflict management and restorative justice heralding peace.
- The Catholic Church needs to be reconciled to herself and present a unified stance to the public.
- Peace building is a long process, an on-going process which calls for engagement despite the many real challenges.
- The moral role of each individual is very important and is the guide to decision making.
- The message of peace need to be spoken and modeled by the Catholic Church.

Rev. John Conway, MM has worked in Africa since 1963. He was the Africa Regional Superior from 1986 - 1992. Currently he is teaching at the Apostles of Jesus Seminary and is involved in chemical dependency rehabiliation programs.

Mission to Justice from a
Healthcare Perspective

Ms. Kathleen J. Dunford, MLM

An important part of my being here started back in the United States
and also in a British Colony where I lived and raised my children from
1975 to 1989. Just to give you a little background: I am a Physician
Assistant, the American equivalent of a Clinical Officer here in Kenya,
and worked as such in the New York and New Jersey areas from 1992
to 2008, after which I joined Maryknoll Lay Missioners.

To me, one of the most important things about this talk is my journey
of faith. I was raised a Catholic by my mother, Mary McGonegal
Jones, a devoted Irish Catholic, who went to church every day. Mary
and Stan Jones lived in New Jersey and had ten children; I was the
fourth oldest. Mother felt a strong responsibility to raise her children
Catholic, even though my father wasn't Catholic. In those days, we
went to church every Sunday, received communion, went to confession,
benediction, Stations of the Cross, crowning of Mary ceremonies,
catechism classes – you name it, and my family was there!

I remember when I was about ten or eleven and looking up at mother
in church and thinking, "Gee, I wish I had that!" She was praying and
in her own spiritual world, and I'm sitting there just bored, bored,
bored. Oh my God, I wanted to go outside, go to the beach, roller
skate, play, anything but to sit in church! And I say that because that
image came back to me later on in my life. I did enjoy the Latin Mass
and any kind of singing, particularly the sung Latin Mass. I was in the
church choir and the high school choir and loved them.

But back to my journey of faith: I was a "fallen away" Catholic from the time I was about 21 into my 40's. I was like St. Paul; I couldn't stand the Catholic Church. It was "don't do this, don't do that," fear and punishment, and I wanted to go my own way – until I hit a wall, namely, I did not have a very good marriage. I became emotionally, physically and certainly, spiritually drained. We Joneses were taught to rely only on ourselves in our big family and stand on our own two feet. And during most of my marriage, I lived far from my family with my husband and two sons. I had two young children, had to work full time, and take care of the house and husband. It was really rough going: I didn't have any support from my husband and had no family around to call upon. And the situation did get worse, to the point where I started going to a support group.

This support group started my journey of faith and learning to lean on God. The defining moment was when a friend of mine brought me to her Methodist church. "Come on, let's go, it's a good church, you'll enjoy it," she said. And it was – the fellowship, the hymns, the sermons were down to earth and relevant to me at the time. I still didn't want anything to do with the Catholic Church because it was, or so I thought, fear producing and ready to punish anyone who stepped out of line just a little.

But one day at the Methodist church, we had just finished a hymn and the minister said to turn and welcome your neighbor and say hello and I turned around. Now this church had a ministry to the mental health hospital down the road and the patients would come every Sunday. So I turned around and there was this Downs Syndrome woman, smiling, innocent, having a great time and wanted to shake my hand eagerly and I just burst out crying. I said "Wow, if this lady who really has no family, no home and lives in a hospital, and has limited intellect, yet she has God looking after her as I could tell by her innocent smile, she is the sparrow that God is taking care of." That showed very much in her face and her smile. I then realized that God could take care of me.

So, that started by real journey of coming back to God. God found me, or I found God through difficult circumstances, or I was open to finding him. This was the biggest thing that ever happened to me in my life, and still is. So, my faith continued to grow and eventually I went back to the Catholic Church after a year or so.

In the early 1990's, I was watching a documentary about Mother Teresa and was just so struck and inspired by the work that she did and her love for Jesus. Through all adversity, she kept persisting in her vocation and work. I said, "Wow, I really want some of what she has": the way she clung to Jesus, clung to God – such wonderful devotion. So, I always kept that dream alive and here I am in 2011 – two years in Kenya, working at a small hospital in the Kitale area under the auspices of the Catholic Diocese of Kitale as a clinical officer.

What God has done in my life has been truly a miracle. I am so grateful that I had my mother's example of faith, and also all the structures of the church. All this I was able to draw upon in my time of need, especially my mother's faith, and has held me in good stead in the good and dark times. God opened a door and let me in, and I am just so grateful to realize that God is not fear and punishment, but love and mercy. So, this leads me into my next topic: What has it been like these last few years as an expatriate missioner working for Maryknoll Lay Missioners and what should expatriate missioners know about the African healthcare system?

Life and Ministry in Kenya

First of all, I have had a wonderful experience with the medical people here in Kenya. I have worked with consultants, medical officers, clinical officers, nurses, and they have been wonderfully helpful, instructive, and knowledgeable in their field. I currently work with two clinical officers both of whom are great guys, work hard, are compassionate and, without reservation, have shared their knowledge of the Kenyan medical system and its approach to treating diseases common to Africa. None of this did I know before I came here; but these two guys were and are always there to help me. I can't praise them enough! I have been working for the past six months at a smaller clinic in the Diocese, and without the knowledge I gained from working with these guys, I could not have taken up these responsibilities. And it's not just the medical knowledge, but the knowledge of Kenyan customs, cultures, and how the healthcare system works here.

Specifically, what I have learned about Kenyan healthcare is illustrated below. There is a large discrepancy between the "haves" and "have-nots" and this is reflected in the area of healthcare. Access to healthcare is limited for the poor, mostly because of poverty. A typical mother of, say, five children, who has one child sick, may wait for five to seven days, hoping that the child will get better on his own, because the mother is torn between feeding her other children vs. paying to see a doctor and buying medicines for the sick child. She may even be faced with the additional problem of the sick child needing to be admitted to the hospital – another "huge" cost, relatively speaking, to the mother. This mother may be a single parent whose husband may have left the family for another woman or greener pastures and, therefore, the mother relies on casual work to support her family; so she is really in a dilemma now with very limited funds and faced with a possible bill from the hospital for a very sick child. Hopefully, she may have family and neighbors who could help out; or she may talk to the hospital administrator and see if there are any charity funds for her sick child. The majority of charity funds come from outside donors. The Government of Kenya does offer free TB and HIV/AIDS treatment and first line malaria drug treatment (that is, if the clinic/ hospital has the drugs available), but a lot of the drugs are funded by outside sources.

Most doctors, clinical officers, and nurses are well trained and are expected to use their training in a very broad way to assist patients in getting well. The professional examination requirements of the Ministry of Health are stringent, and a healthcare worker comes out of school well trained. However (and a big however), the infrastructure in most Government hospitals is poor – two or three patients to a bed, overcrowding, limited professional staff, lack of essential drugs many times in the pharmacies and outmoded equipment. Once a family member is admitted to a government hospital, families are given a list of drugs and injections to buy at an outside pharmacy, incurring much higher costs. The queues are very long at most Government facilities, and it takes the patience of a saint to spend a whole day with a crying, sick baby to wait for a doctor to see you. This is also a very big strain on the medical profession. If one has enough money, you can buy great health care with the best of hospitals, specialists, and modern testing and equipment. So Kenya has the medical personnel to give good healthcare, but unfortunately, not the infrastructure to do so yet, and I say "yet" because Kenya is still a young country as far as medical infrastructure is concerned (when you think that only 50 years ago it became independent, and only in the last twenty years has it had any type of numbers in the way of medical officers, clinical officers, and nurses to help its citizens). But I don't think it will take just money, money, money to solve the medical problems of Kenya; it will take good care, good organization, good administration, and accountability on the financial side.

At Kiminini Cottage Hospital and also St. Raphael's Dispensary at Matisi we have been able to help many patients with outside donor money. For example, in the last two years, many young children have had their cleft lips and palates repaired successfully at Kijabe Hospital. We provided transport, food costs and lodging for them and their mothers to go to the hospital in Nairobi and to bring them back all smiles.

Similarly, we are treating a 16 year old teenager who has a poorly functioning heart because of Rheumatic Heart Disease (RHD) acquired several years ago. Her disease is so bad that she can't walk half a block without being exhausted. She looks like she is only 7 years old because her growth has been so stunted by her heart disease. Another patient is a 38 years old single mother of two children who had to quit her job in Eldoret because she also has a diseased heart, again because of RHD as a teenager. Both people come to us for help – medically, emotionally, spiritually, and financially because the cost of a heart valve replacement under normal circumstances is in the area of 800,000 Ksh. We were able to find a program through the MEAK (Medical and Education Aid to Kenya) program that will replace their diseased heart valves for free by UK doctors in conjunction with Kenyatta National Hospital (KNH). This will cost us 20,000 shillings besides transport and lodging for each of these patients. There are many such stories in Kenya.

In another case, a desperate mother came to us at Matisi Clinic with her three-month old daughter. Her spinal cord had not closed properly *in utero* and she had part of it coming out of her neck (similar to *spina bifida* but in the neck). Since this was an urgent matter, we were able to send her for assessment by the Kijabe doctors who booked her right away for surgery. Now she has had her surgery and she is a fine healthy child, neurologically intact and growing very well. While we can only help one patient at a time, we are helping, and I am grateful to be able to help.

Concluding Remarks

What have I learned from being here? To have an open mind, not to judge people and things by Western standards, but to live in the reality of life here in Kenya and, most of all, to keep the faith! The Kenyan people have taught me to be more compassionate, more giving, more loving – not just because they are poor and in need, but because they persevere in the face of many obstacles and struggles, particularly the mothers and children. They are very grateful for the care given; "*Nashukuru,*" (I am grateful), I hear many of them say and for any small kindness given. It is not my giving, but rather my receiving many blessings from them and the privilege of sharing their ups and downs with them. "*Sina pesa*" (I have no money) is a phrase I hear often, and indeed it is often the case where a helping hand is needed to bridge the gap between the haves and have-nots.

Another question is put to me: Is healthcare a right in Kenya? Well, Kenya has a way to go before universal healthcare is available to all its citizens. A step in the right direction is the Government's National Health Insurance Fund (NHIF), where people voluntarily contribute monthly amounts of money to ensure against healthcare expenditures. For example, right now, a citizen can contribute Ksh 160 per month, and for that they or any member of their immediate family can be treated for free by an approved hospital (prearranged daily charge) – government, mission, or private. This is a really good deal in healthcare, especially for rural areas! Unfortunately, a lot of people cannot afford the 160 Ksh per month, or don't know how it works or that it even exists!

Another reason that some people don't sign up for NHIF is that they weigh paying the monthly premiums vs. feeding their families every day. Most people in Kenya, especially in the rural areas where I live, live on only Ksh 100 a day! So what would you do as a mother or father? As a mother, I would probably address the immediate need of feeding the family, and hope for the best if my child gets sick. Of course, this is where faith in God comes in. My mother had ten children and I remember her talking to me when I was in my twenties when I asked her how she and Dad were going to manage educating the rest of the kids (I was fourth oldest), and she said simply, "God will provide." Well, not having the faith of my mother at that time, I thought she was crazy, but in fact they did manage to feed, clothe, shelter, and educate a family of ten! I think a lot of this type of faith goes on in Kenya, especially with the women. There are many instances where a parent tells me that "God will provide" and "God will bless us."

But back to the NHIF: there are several other insurance companies that offer healthcare coverage, but NHIF is probably the cheapest and it is now thinking of offering insurance for outpatient services. They already offer insurance for inpatient and maternity care. I am hoping this will change the face of healthcare in Kenya. Another idea would be to offer special discount coverage for people with chronic diseases like asthma, Sickle Cell disease, diabetes, hypertension, and so on. I also think it would be good for hospitals to cover the elderly in much the same way government hospitals do not charge for room and board for children under five. The working population could then contribute according to their wages to support these two special, needy categories as well as themselves generally and their families.

Health may be a right, but it is also a responsibility. Just as in the USA, Kenyans need to know that if they do have high blood pressure, diabetes, or asthma, that they need to make the lifestyle changes necessary to control their conditions. A diabetic who does not take his medicine, does not follow any diet, and does not exercise cannot expect to demand healthcare as a right if he is not doing his part. All these abuses of the body and mind take its toll on a person, and often not only is the person affected, but the family suffers sometimes more than the patient. All people need to understand that they can contribute to their health and this is called healthcare responsibility.

How about African missioners going to the First World? What can they offer? Plenty! Consumerism is so rampant in the USA, and the simple, but real, life in Kenya could teach Americans the real values of family life and love. Also the Kenyan's example of faith in God could help a lot of the Western world return to God and rely on Him rather being so independent – just like I was before finding God. Kenyans need to appreciate what they have to offer the rest of the world. In conclusion, I am very glad to be here and to tell you of my experiences. Blessings on all of you.

Ms. Kathleen J. Dunford is Maryknoll Lay Missioner working in Kitale, Kenya. She is a qualified clinical nurse.

The Environment and the Integrity of Creation

Rev. Kenneth Thesing, MM

We read stories on the environment each day in our daily newspapers. And these stories will continue to appear in the future because we are all aware in our lives now of issues of the environment; we have interest and look for more information.

And so what I want for us here today as we speak about the Environment is to *situate* ourselves as *"church people,"* as people of faith. That is my goal and purpose in this short presentation. I want to set out some principles from which we can continue our conversation.

"If you want to cultivate peace, protect creation"

This is the title of Pope Benedict XVI's message for the celebration of the World Day of Peace on1 January 2010.[1] Respect for creation, the Pope said, is immensely important because "creation is the beginning and the foundation of all God's works."[2] Many threats arise from the neglect, even misuse of the earth and the natural goods God has given us. Therefore, humankind, all peoples, must renew and strengthen "the covenant between human beings and the environment."[3]

Pope Benedict stated in his encyclical, *Caritas in Veritate* (2009, no. 48) that the environment must be seen as God's gift to all people, and

---

1 All church document references can be freely accessed on and downloaded from the Vatican website: www.vatican.va

2 *Catechism of the Catholic Church* (CCC), no. 198.

3 Benedict XVI, "Message for the World Day of Peace, 2008, no 7.

the use we make of it entails a shared responsibility for all humanity, including future generations. And, he says, seeing creation as God's gift to humanity helps us understand our vocation and worth as human beings. Psalm 8:4-5 says: "When I look at your heavens, at the work of your hands, the moon and the stars which you have established; *what is man* (humankind) that you are mindful of him/them and the son of man that you care for him/them?" Twenty one years ago, Pope John Paul II in his 1990 Message for the World Day of Peace (no. 1) said that "ecological awareness...needs to be helped to develop and mature, and find fitting expression in concrete programmes and initiatives." And forty years ago in 1971, Pope Paul VI, in his encyclical letter *Octogesima Adveniens* (no. 21) pointed out that "by an ill-considered exploitation of nature (humankind) risks destroying it and becoming in his turn the victim of this degradation ... Not only is the material environment becoming a permanent menace – pollution and refuse, new illnesses and absolute destructive capacity – but the human framework is no longer under humankind's control, thus creating an environment for tomorrow which may well be intolerable. This is a wide-ranging social problem which concerns the entire human family."

Pope Benedict says that without entering into the realm of specific technical solutions to concrete environmental concerns (because as Church, the Church has no special technical expertise), the Church, as an "expert in humanity," is concerned to call attention to the relationship between the Creator, human beings and the created order. He mentioned that in 1990 Pope John Paul had pointed to the "urgent moral need for a new solidarity," that is, an understanding that we human beings all over the earth cannot remain indifferent before the problems associated with such realities as climate change, desertification, the deterioration and loss of productivity in vast agricultural areas, the pollution of rivers, the loss of biodiversity, the increase of natural catastrophes and ...deforestation."

And, therefore, Pope Benedict says we must look at our models of development as well as at our cultural values and understand that our present crises – be they environmental or economic or food-related (famine and lack of food security), or social – are ultimately also moral crises, and all of them are interrelated. They call us to solidarity with all people and to discern new ways and strategic planning for all to live together now, and also to a renewed sense of intergenerational solidarity: We have inherited from past generations, and we have benefitted from the work of our contemporaries; for this reason we have obligations towards all, and we can not refuse to interest ourselves in those who will come after us."[4]

In this regard, Pope Benedict says it is all too clear that large numbers of people in different countries are experiencing increased hardship because of the negligence or refusal of many others to exercise responsible stewardship over the environment. Here each of us can examine our own personal activities in how we treat the environment. We all, and individually, says the Pope, can no longer do without a real change of outlook which will result in new life-styles. We are all responsible for the protection and care of the environment; we cannot remain indifferent to what is happening around us.

The Church, says Pope Benedict in the encyclical letter *Caritas in Veritate* (no. 51), has a responsibility towards creation just as it does toward the human person, considered individually and in relation to others. For this reason the Church encourages efforts to promote a greater sense of ecological responsibility; for at one and the same time this affirms the inviolability of human life at every stage, and in every condition reaffirms the dignity of the human person and the human family and safeguards the legacy of human society. And so Pope Benedict recalls the biblical teaching that Christ, crucified and risen, has bestowed his spirit of holiness upon humankind, to guide the course of history in anticipation of that day when, with the return of Christ, there will be "new heavens and a new earth" (2 Pet 3:13). Protecting the environment in order to build a world of peace is, therefore. a duty given to each of us, a challenge we face with renewed commitment and an opportunity to hand down to coming generations the prospect of a better future for all.

Therefore: If you want to cultivate peace, protect creation.

---

4 Paul VI, *Populorum Progressio*, no. 17.

Recommendations

What then do we do? First we can study and learn about The Social Teachings of the Catholic Church on environment: *The Compedium of the Social Doctrine of the Church.* This is now available in the Catholic Bookshop here in Nairobi, as a Paulines Publication. The book comes with a complete index enabling you to quickly locate a theme or topic and see references to it in the *Catechism of the Catholic Church* and all the papal encyclicals and talks of the popes. Also all materials are available for free access and downloading on the Catholic Church website www.vatican.va

Secondly, here in Kenya the Catholic Church, through its various departments and programs has been active in various ways to foster awareness and action in the area of environment:

(a)   The Kenyan Church Lenten Campaign, through the Kenyan Episcopal Conference Justice and Peace Office, each year since 2004 has focused at least one week on an aspect of the environment.

(b)   The Kenya Caritas Office, the Association of Sisters' Congregations in Kenya (AOSK), and Kenya Catholic Relief Services (CRS) all plan and implement programs each year on aspects related to the environment.

(c)   Ukweli Video (Earthkeepers), AMECEA/Cafod (In Search of Better Governance), Caritas/CRS (Weaving Peace in the Rift Valley, the Sand Dams of Kitui) have produced videos on environmental issues in Kenya.

(d)   There are many secular Kenyan non-governmental organizations (NGOs) and Civil Society Organizations (CSOs) to contact which work on various aspects of land, water, conflict resolution, and so on, related to issues that arise from our living together in creation and our living in relationship, positively and negatively, with the environment.

(e)   The new Kenya Constitution has a section on land, Chapter 5, also on the environment.

So, what then do we do? "The Urgent need is not for churches as churches to enter the political fray (although they must take a moral stand) but for Christians as citizens to exercise their renewed consciences and contact decision makers."[5]

So we form ourselves and, as ministers in the Church, we form the whole church and society to be also in service to our environment.

Summary of the Main Issues

- We really need to get the Church Social Teaching to the grassroots, that is, so that it begins to affect our church at the parish and Small Christian Community (SCC) level. But what we have experienced in this talk has exposed us to how relevant the church documents are if we are aware of them and know how to take out of them the parts that relate to our local concerns.

- We really need to get practical when we start to talk about and use the Social Teaching documents of the church. As the previous person said, there is so much there that can help us with our local situations if we know how to relate that material to our situations.

- I reflect from the talk how much we *depend* on the environment: "We need the egg more than the egg needs us." That is a phrase I use to illustrate this. I realize we each need to do our own small things at our local level in terms of caring for the environment, and it builds up throughout the community. We are all interdependent in reference to the environment because, either positively or negatively, what each one does affects all the others. I never thought so much before of the interconnectivity of it all.

- We grew up thinking we are "over" the environment; that is, our human position was one of dominance. Now we have learned not to be "over" the environment, not to even be "stewards" of creation, but to be part of it. And that brings both understanding of

---

5 Bread for the World, Lutheran Church Advocacy and Education Organization, Washington, DC, USA

and the recognition by us now that much of creation is suffering and we are suffering because of environmental negligence.

- It was so important to hear the references to a "new solidarity." I am thinking now of the parable: "Treat the earth well; it was not given to you by your parents; it was loaned to you by your children." This teaches us intergenerational solidarity.

- Integration also was an important word for me to hear, and I reflect now on how we must learn always to integrate all the aspects on environment or creation, be it the care of land, of water, of air, of the crops, the animals and humans, and even the minerals. I say this because they affect each other. All that is a part of life must be held as if in the palm of the hand.

- I see a lack of networking by all of the organizations; there is a lot going on, even in our country here in Kenya, as we heard. But it all seems to be done without a common purpose, and maybe we could be so much more effective through more consciously working together, networking.

- I have a question with regard schools: we have secular and Catholic schools. What voice does the Catholic Church have, or raise, or exercise, in this area of environment or creation? In response one person said the Church must play a prophetic, kingly and priestly role.

- I see the problem with environment or, let us say, climate change this way: governments meet at Copenhagen, for example, and they pass resolutions, but these too go nowhere or are ineffective unless in the countries themselves there are movements or groups that bring pressure to get legislation and regulations and enforcement of these resolutions.

- One thing is clear; this is a very big issue. The awareness now is with us all, that environment and climate change is affecting us all, even in countries, like here in Africa, that are only now beginning to have much impact on the overall world climate. But we see how we are already deeply affected, as our rain patterns change, our rivers and water sources are different, some drying up. So, I see that it is crucial that we all say that all of us must be involved, starting with myself, my community, my society, and then move on to work to effect change at greater levels.

Conclusions

Solidarity: how do we use Catholic Social Teaching which is there for us, and have it become real and effective at the local level?

Recycling: it must start with each one of us, start with our own kitchen, our own farm, our own "egg."

We are part of creation, not over it. Through our SCCs or whatever way we have locally, we must get our Church documents and teaching to be alive and effective at our local level. Never forget to keep it local: think globally but act at the local level.

Rev. Kenneth Thesing, MM has worked in parochial ministry, the training of lay leaders and the promotion of personal and civic growth among the people through various projects in agriculture, health and education in Kenya, Tanzania, Sudan, Mozambique. He has also served as the General Superior for the Maryknoll Society. Currently, he is involved in peace and justice programs in Africa.

Break-out Discussion Group Report on the Environment and Integrity of Creation

Sister Sia Temu, MM

"If you want to cultivate peace, protect creation." Pope Benedict XVI, World Day of Peace Message, 1 January 2010.

"... [C]reation is the beginning and the foundation of all God's works,". *Catechism of the Catholic Church, #198.*

Therefore humankind must renew and strengthen "the covenant between human beings and the environment." Benedict XVI, 2008 World Day of Peace Message, #7.

Benedict XVI, *Caritas in Veritate*, 2009, #48: the environment must be seen as God's gift to all people.

Psalm 8:4-5 on our vocation and worth as human beings: "When I look at your heavens, at the work of your hands, the moon and the stars which you have established, what is man (humankind) that you are mindful of him (them), that you...care for him (them)."

Pope John Paul II, 1990 World Day of Peace Message, #1: "[E] cological awareness ... needs to be helped to develop and mature, and find fitting expression in concrete programs and initiatives."

Pope Paul VI, *Octogesima Adveniens,* 1971, #21: "[B]y an ill-considered exploitation of nature (humankind) risks destroying it and becoming in turn the victim of this degradation..."

The Church has no special technological expertise on environmental concerns, but, says Benedict XVI, the Church as an "expert in humanity" calls attention to the relationship between the Creator, human beings and the created order. There is an "urgent moral need for a new solidarity" to the problems associated with environmental deterioration.

Therefore we must look at our models of development as well as our cultural values. We are called to solidarity with all people and between and among generations: "... [W]e cannot refuse to interest ourselves in those who will come after us," Pope Paul VI, *Populorum Progressio*, 1967, #17.

Large numbers of people in different countries suffer because of environmental negligence. This calls us to a real change of outlook leading to new life-styles

The Church has a responsibility toward creation just as it does toward the human person (*Caritas in Veritate*, #51). This reaffirms the dignity of the human person and the human family and safeguards the legacy of human society.

Pope Benedict recalls the biblical teaching that Christ, crucified and risen, has bestowed his spirit of holiness upon humankind, to guide the course of history until that day when, with the return of Christ, there will be "new heavens and a new earth" (2 Pet. 3:13).

Protecting the environment is therefore a duty given to each of us, a challenge we face, and an opportunity to hand down to coming generations the prospect of a better future for all. Therefore, "If you want to cultivate peace, protect creation."

What Then Do We Do?

Study and learn about the Social Teachings of the Catholic Church on environment: (a) the Papal Encyclicals, (b) The Catechism of the Catholic Church (c) Pope Benedict's talks, (d) all materials are available for free access and downloading on the Catholic Church website www.vatican.va.

Here in Kenya the Catholic Church through its various departments and program has been active in various ways to foster awareness and action in the area of Environment:

The Kenyan Church Lenten Campaign, through the Justice and Peace Office of the Kenya Bishops' Conference, each year since 2004 has focused at least one week on an aspect of the Environment.

The Kenya Caritas Office, The Association of Sisters (Congregations) in Kenya (AOSK) and Kenya Catholic Relief Services all plan and implement programs each year on aspects related to the Environment (land, water, conflict, etc.).

Ukweli Video (Earthkeepers), AMECEA/Cafod (In Search of Better Governance), Caritas/CRS (Weaving Peace in the Rift Valley, The Sand Dams of Kitui) have produced videos on environmental issues in Kenya.

There are many secular Kenyan non-governmental organizations (NGOs) and civil society organizations (CSOs) one can contact which work on various aspects of land, water, conflict resolution, etc., related to issues that arise from our living together in creation and our living in relationship, positively and negatively, with the environment.

So, what then do we do? "The urgent need is not for churches as churches to enter the political fray (although they must take a moral stand) but for Christians as citizens to exercise their renewed consciences and contact decision makers" Bread for the World (A US Based Lutheran Church Advocacy and Education for Action Group).

Sister Sia Temu, MM, a Maryknoll sister, works on peace-building and conflict transformation as part of a Maryknoll Sisters peace team in Africa based in Nairobi, Kenya.

PART II
MISSION "AD GENTES"
Greetings

Sister Teresa Hougnon, MM

Good morning! Welcome to our second day of the Maryknoll Mission Symposium. My name is Sister Teresa Hougnon, a Maryknoll Sister. Please join me in prayer:

God Creator, you have accompanied us through the ages, bringing us to this moment in time. One hundred years is like a second for you. But in your Graciousness, you have blessed us in mission, with life and abundance in Africa, as we all trace our roots to Africa. We remember all those who have gone before us. And we pray that your gifts may be revealed through our work and our sharing. Amen.

Our discussions yesterday afternoon were on Mission and Justice, Economics, Peace, Environment, and Medical Issues. Today we move to Mission ad Gentes – reaching out to others. We will hear from three missioners about their experiences in the field, followed by break out discussion groups with each presenting missioner.

Sister Teresa Hougnon, MM, a Maryknoll sister, works on peace-building and conflict transformation as part of a Maryknoll Sisters peace team in Africa based in Nairobi, Kenya.

A Christian among Moslems

Augustin Sawadogo, MAfr

This is a testimony of my experience with Moslems in Khartoum, Sudan, during my two years of pastoral work from 2006 to 2008. When I arrived in Khartoum I was much impressed by the fact that everything was in Arabic, starting from billboards and sign posts to public notices. I noticed quickly also the strict gender separation in public gatherings. At my parish, Arabic was the language used for every single activity. We only spoke English in community or with other religious missionaries. So, the challenge of knowing Arabic was so obvious that I needed nobody to tell me I should put the necessary energy to learn it as fast as possible. Even though the knowledge of the language was necessary for my insertion in the local community, my physical features were of a typical Sudanese, and this was a big advantage.

During my two years experience, in the beginning I learnt the Sudanese spoken Arabic which helped me carry out my ordinary responsibilities such as being the local bursar of my community. So, I used to go to the local open market to buy food for the house and other items for upkeep. In the market and anywhere at any time the starting point is the greeting: "*as-salam aleikum,*" which means, peace be upon you (plural, because each person has two angels, the bad and the good and both of them should be greeted with the person). One day as I was walking in the market looking for items to buy, I could hear people calling me: "*yaa Mohammad! yaa Mohammad*"! This was to get my attention as they named me after the prophet Mohammad. The tradition is to name after the prophet Mohammad any male person whose name is unknown. But I had no clue what it meant and was embarrassed. A number of times as community we were invited to attend wedding ceremonies and other religious feasts. I could see a couple of time people washing their hands before meals; however, very often they do not. People feel comfortable in sharing meals from the same plate in groups of five or more without washing the hands. They do not see it as necessary. What is important is to say: *"bismi lahi,"* to mean "In the name of God." When I asked, I was told that among brothers all are clean and God protects. During Ramadan, the fasting month, people break their fast together or are obliged to do so wherever they find themselves at the time of breaking the fast. This is because extra food is always provided and it is a blessing to have someone break their fast with you; there is no checking whether one is fasting or not. Often, I had nice meals around the market place whenever I went for my usual shopping.

At the University

I spent one academic year in an Islamic university in the mornings, learning the Arabic language and Islamic faith and culture. In the afternoon I would go for pastoral work among the Christians of my parish. Before I started the studies, I had to explicitly inform the registration office that I was a Christian since they could suspect me of being a spy. Thanks to a fellow Burkinabe who was studying there I was granted the permission. I was very happy but fearful as well. When I started the classes, one question loomed always in my head and always increased my fear. It was how would my class mates and others react once they discovered that I am a Christian who is not willing to convert to Islam? To make myself confident, I tried to ask myself the craziest questions I could imagine they might ask me, and I tried to find an adequate answer to each question.

I used public transport to go to school and during my journeys in the bus everybody was quiet and everything was very respectful and religious. There was no entertainment with profane music such as rhythm and blues (R'n'B) and other flavours apart from radio stations broadcasting news and religious songs, or most often the Qur`an being chanted.

At the language institute we studied many subjects, among which the Qur`an. This class consisted most of the time in reciting and reading aloud the Qur`an. The teacher would randomly go around asking anybody to recite a part or the whole of a chapter (*sura)* that himself chooses, since most of the students had memorised the Qur`an before coming to learn the language. One day in his movement I happened to be the person of his choice. He asked me to recite one *sura* which I did not know, then he asked me two other different ones which I did not know either. At last he asked me the *sura al- Faatiha* which, in comparison, would be the Our Father for a Catholic. To his big surprise I did not know this one either. He asked me then: Do you pray? To this, I kept quiet because some Moslems think that Christians do not pray, so if I answered yes I am saying that I am a Moslem, and if I say no I am confirming their thought that Christians do not pray since soon or later they will know I am a Christian. He continued: do you go to the mosque? I kept quiet still because answering no would be a scandal or an attitude of lack of respect for them. He realised that I had decided not to answer these questions. So he asked me again: Are you a Christian? To this, my answer was yes. Then suddenly he said: Oh! I now understand. Then he said to me: Let me teach you a *sura.* The chapter is called *al-kaafirun,* which means the infidels. He asked me to repeat it after him as it follows:

قُلْ يَأَيُّهَا ٱلْكَـٰفِرُونَ

Say (O Muhammad): O ye who reject faith! (1)

لَا أَعْبُدُ مَا تَعْبُدُونَ

I worship not that which ye worship. (2)

وَلَا أَنتُمْ عَـٰبِدُونَ مَا أَعْبُدُ

Nor will you worship that which I worship. (3)

وَلَا أَنَا عَابِدٌ مَّا عَبَدتُّمْ

And I will never worship that which you worship. (4)

وَلَا أَنتُمْ عَـٰبِدُونَ مَا أَعْبُدُ

Nor will you worship that which I worship. (5)

لَكُمْ دِينُكُمْ وَلِىَ دِينِ

Unto you, is your religion and unto me is my religion (Islam). (6)

After this exercise, he asked a volunteer who knew the meaning of the chapter to translate it into English for me since at that time my Arabic was not strong enough to understand the Arabic text. A Somali proposed himself and for the first sentence he rather said: "O! Say you Christians." To my surprise, the whole class reacted against him, saying: "Do not say 'Christians' but infidels or disbelievers." Then the translator immediately apologised to me and at the end of the class he again talked to me saying: "I did not have any bad intention against you, I am really sorry." I accepted his apology once more and assured him that I will not keep a grudge. In fact, according to me, he had translated exactly what all the rest had in the back of their minds since, for many Muslims, all non-Muslim believers are infidels. I was not surprised at all that he translated it that way; I was rather astonished that the whole class reacted against his translation. Finally, this was the day I feared would soon arrive; now I had to be firm but "diplomatic" in gentleness and in expressing my Catholic convictions. Almost everyone came to know that I was a Christian. However, surprisingly, they all became friendlier to me than before. Surely, the intention was to convert me. Many would invite me to the mosque for prayers because the first afternoon prayer was before the end of our classes and everybody went for prayer except me. I was strict on my position. If I go to the mosque even once, I would give them false hope that I may convert to Islam. So, I never went to the mosque with them for prayer but at the request of some of my classmates, I used to take the ablutions before the Qur'an class for purity purpose. Some asked me why I rejected Islam since I am a learned and good person. Some told me that I am a wonderful person but, unfortunately, I am lost and will be sent to hell if I do not convert before death. To defend my Catholic faith, I always used this *hadith* called *al-muflis* (المفلس,), which means the bankrupt:

The prophet (peace be upon him) asked his companions, "do you know who is the bankrupt?" His companions replied": "the bankrupt among us is one who has neither money nor property." The prophet (peace be upon him) said: "the real bankrupt of my community *(ummah)* would be he who would come on the day of resurrection with much of prayer, fasting, and *sadaqah;* but he will find himself bankrupt on that day as he will have exhausted the funds of virtues because he reviled others, brought calumny against others, unlawfully devoured the wealth of others, shed the blood of others, and beat others, so his virtues would be credited to the account of those who suffered at his hand, if his good deeds fall short to clear the account, their sins would be entered in his account and he would be thrown in the hellfire.

وه نم نوفرعت له" : هباحصأ (ملس و هيلع هللا ىلص) يبنلا لأس الو لاملا كلمي ال يذلا وه اننيب سلفملا" هباحصأ باجأو "؟سلفملا يتمأ نم سلفملا نإ"لاق (ملسو هيلع هللا ىلص) يبنلا ."ةيكلملا ةالصلا نم ريثكلاب موي يتأي فوس يذلا وه نوكي يقيقحلا هنأل موي لا كلذ يف ةسلفم هسفن دجيس هنكلو ،ةقدصلاو ،مايصلاو ، بلج ،نيرخآلا متش هنأل لئاضفلا نم لاومألا تدفنتسا دق نوكتس كفسو ،نيرخآلا تاورث مهتلي ةعورشم ريغ ةروصب ،ءارتفا نيرخآلا باسح ىلع هلئاضف لضفلاب نوكيس كلذل ،نيرخآلا زافو ،نيرخآلا مد نوكيس ،باسح حسمل ىقرتل ال هتانسح اذإو ، هدي يف اونع نيذلا كئلوأ لخد اياطخ يف مهباسح، فوسو به يف يقلا به يف منهجلا"

There is a second *hadith* I used to use to support my position; it is known as the believer (*al-mu'min:* نمؤملا) and it says:

Anybody who believes in God and the Last Day should not harm his neighbour, and anybody who believes in God and the Last Day should entertain his guest generously, and anybody who believes in God and the Last Day should talk what is good or keep quiet (i.e. abstain from all kinds of evil and dirty talk).

"كل نم نمؤي باللها ويلاو رخآلا ينغبني نأ ال يضري هراج، وأدح يمؤن باللها ويلاو رخآلا ينغبني فرتي هفيض فيضب هناخس،ءاو أود نمؤي باللها ويلاو رخآلا نأ لحدثي ام وه ديج وأ لينصمت (يأ ال نتماع نع كل اونع يف رشلا نقاش وقذرف) ،كذرت ينبلا دمحم (ص) يف ثيدح يبأ هريره يف 47. ثيدح 8 :لمجلا، يراخبلا حيحص صص

With these two *hadiths* I make a connection to what Jesus said concerning the love-commandment: "Jesus answered, The first is, 'Hear, O Israel: The Lord our God, the Lord is one; and you shall love the Lord your God with all your heart, and with all your soul, and with all your mind, and with all your strength.' The second is this, 'You shall love your neighbour as yourself.' There is no other commandment greater than these." (Mk12:29-31). There were many of my classmates who came to visit me and my community in my parish where I had my normal pastoral activities with the youth (music group and YCS) and Small Christian Community.

My second major experience to talk about happened during a class of oral expression. During this class every student was supposed to introduce himself to the rest of the class while standing in front. At the end of the introduction, each was expected to say: *"wa al-hamdulillah ana Moslim,"* which means, "and praise be to God I am a Moslem". At my turn, I felt a strong uneasiness that my neighbour sensed and said to me: "Not worry, just go and introduce yourself." I introduced myself and ended in saying simply: "I am a Christian." The class became quiet but nothing still changed in our relationship; everything went very well, more than I could expect.

The third and last experience concerns an SMS I received as a wish on Christmas day. It was sent by the person who helped me for my registration at the University a Burkinabe Muslim and good friend. The SMS was the entire short *sura* that says: "Say: He is Allah, the One Allah, the Eternal, Absolute; He begetteth not, nor is He begotten; and there is none like unto Him." The Arabic text is:

بسم الله الرحمن الرحيم
قل هو الله أحدۙ١
الله الصّمد٢
لم يلد ولم يولدۙ٣
ولم يكن لّه كفوًا أحد٤

If a Muslim and friend sends such an SMS to his Christian friend on Christmas, the message is clear. The more I learnt about Islam the more the stereotypes I had of Islam dissipated and the more naturally I defended them. This made my superiors suspect that I was on my way to converting to Islam. So, they decided among themselves to stop me from finishing the studies. Fortunately, by the grace of God, the one who was charged with breaking the news to me never had the courage to do so until I finished studies. They only told me when they presented my pastoral report to me at the end of my stay in Khartoum. I had no intension of becoming a Muslim. I did not find anything fundamental about the faith that is not in Christianity, though I admire Islam and respect it. The fundamental change that happened in me is my love for saying Muslim blessings and wishes and the ability to put on a Muslim garment and hat publicly and comfortably. These are things I never thought could happen to me. I had many other human experiences with Muslims and Arabs. They were beautiful and faith constructing experiences that will mark my whole life forever. For this I am grateful to my superiors who helped me to have this experience that I find unique in my missionary formation.

Moreover, I could easily link all these experiences to my experience as a child, born in a Christian family from a mixed society of African traditional religious persons and Muslims in Burkina Faso. This helped and facilitated the integration of my pastoral experience into my own faith journey of seeking more understanding in relation to believers of other religions, especially Islam. To conclude, as someone said, instead of fighting to show that God is one`s side let us struggle to be on the side of God.

Augustine Sawadogo is a Missionaries of Africa seminarian. He is in his third year of theology in Tangaza College.

Break-out Discussion Group on Inter-religious Dialogue

Report by Participants

Resume of Presentation

The Presenter began by a Christian greeting in Arabic. It was stated that the presentation would base itself on the speaker's pastoral experience. It was noted that the first striking impression was the ubiquitous Arabic language, in public service vehicles, in the market place, and virtually everywhere a gathering of people was. Being the *lingua franca*, the speaker had to acquaint himself with at least colloquial Arabic.

Market Place

"*Ya Mohammed*," a phrase used by the locals to refer to the speaker was striking. It was realized that such a phrase was used of an individual with whom one was not yet acquainted, i.e. any "John Doe." The manner of greeting, "*a salaam aleikum*" had a religious connotation. It was understood that each individual possessed a set of two spirits, one evil and the other good. This called for a collective greeting lest one of the spirits felt ignored and decided to go apoplectic.

University

Here, the presenter engaged in studies in literal Arabic for one and a half months. All courses offered included Islamic Studies. It was noted that in the Qur'an classes, the lecturer could randomly request a student to recite a *Sura*. This was a source of apprehension on the part of the speaker. It could be discovered he is Christian. Such an instance arose when the speaker was unable to recite the most basic *Sura* – the *Al-fatiha*. Fortunately, his fears were uncalled for. The lecturer, offered to teach him. It was observed that identifying oneself as Christian from the outset eased interaction.

Nevertheless, confrontational instances on religious positions, though subtle, arose. A number were mentioned;

While being introduced to a *Sura,* a fellow student was asked to translate a line from Arabic to English. The student-translator rendered "See you disbelievers" as "See you Christians ..."

The presenter received a Qur'an message on Christmas that seemed to attack the concept of the birth of Christ as God and Son of God: "Say he Allah who is one, he neither begets, nor he's born ..."

Questions such as: "You seem like a nice person and you have good behavior, *but* why are you Christian?

Toward the close of the presentation, the concept of the Christian Golden Rule was discussed in relation to the notion of individual bankruptcy in the *Hadith*. The presentation concluded on a note of encouragement. We should strive to identify common points between religions such as Islam and Christianity to foster harmony.

Break-out Group Discussion Report

A number of points were addressed to the presenter:
What would you consider the fundamental change in yourself?

The presenter observed that he has no problem saying *Bismilahi Rahman Rahim.* He has developed an understanding of what the phrase means. Morever, his attire (he was clad in standard Islamic garb portraying acceptance) reminded him of his native Burkina Faso Muslims.

How would you comment on factions in Islam that are supposedly anti-Christian?

The presenter concurred that these, regrettably, do get more attention than the welcoming ones that played host to him. On this point, he reiterated the need to dwell on a theological rather than a literal interpretation of Holy Scriptures. In attempting to understand such factions as those in question, Christians should understand that at one point in history, hostility was meted out by those who professed Christianity.

Islam is taken as a religion and lifestyle. How can this be understood?

Islam is a religion hinging on the notion of revelation. Other religions (if any, from an Islamic viewpoint) are untrue since they are a distortion of the original message of which Islam is the custodian. Arabic, as a language, portrays an avenue of the expression of this lifestyle.

Does Islam advance any novel aspect to humanity?

Simply put, no.

All of us are supposedly born Muslims. What's your reaction to this claim?

Such a position involves a belief that Adam was Muslim. *Al-kafirun* (non-Muslims) are those who separated from the truth.

Christian Presence Among Marginalized Groups in Northern Kenya

Mr. Felix Nzioka Ngao, CLM

I am a member of the Catholic Lay Missionaries of Kenya (CLM). CLM is an organisation of professionally qualified Catholic lay men and women, single and married, who offer their services for a minimum of two years to the mission of the church, particularly in the marginalized areas in the North and amongst the urban poor in Kenya.

CLM aims at serving the poor and the marginalized, collaborating with them to recognise their God given potential, to also assist people to whom we are sent become self-reliant and missionaries themselves. We also wish to witness to good Christian living.

Our objective is to provide well qualified, motivated personnel for Catholic projects among the pastrolist communities and among the urban poor, to participate in local pastoral activities, to make a positive contribution to the lives of those who are generally forgotten, ignored and are most vulnerable to the uncertainties of economics, national and international politics and the ambition of selfish and unjust men and women. People need to be called in order to respond, and so CLM provides a vehicle through which Kenyan professionals may be called to put into practice their desire to serve the marginalized. We encourage Kenyans to work for a more just and equitable society, to stand firm against corruption and to promote good governance.

I joined CLM 8 years ago and was sent to work in North Horr Parish of Marsabit Diocese. I met and worked with Fidei Donum priests of the Auxberge Diocese of Germany. They have been there for over 40 years, actually as old as the diocese itself.

I am a trained teacher, and naturally was sent to teach in the local secondary school. Of interest is the fact that the school is a public institution that is supposed to be run and managed by the state. Back then, North Horr Boys' was the only secondary school and so girls had to go to Maikona, which is over 40 kilometres away which, translates to a day's journey with "perfect" means.

I wish to now share with you my experience as a Christian among the Gabbra, Borana, Wata, Turkana, and the Dasenach people.

My experience in the North

When I was going through my formation to join CLM, I was told I was going to share my faith with the people. However, just like most Christians, I did not see how that was possible, and so I went there with a certain mindset. To me, I was going to "introduce" God to these people. I had been brought up in the "correct" faith, and this is what I was taking to the people. After all, it is the same faith that was moving me to do I was doing. That unfortunately meant I spent quite a long time looking disapprovingly at how the Catholic Christian faith was practiced by the people.

As a Kenyan from "down country" I did, too, go with an idea that the way "we" had embraced Christianity was how it ought to be. Therefore, at first, I did take issue with how the people from the North embrace their Christian faith vis-à-vis their culture. Luckily for me, the desert is a place of quiet nights and it offers endless space to walk and reflect during the day, and so I was transformed and begun to see things from a different perspective.

There were occasions I felt caught up. There were on the one hand the local people and, as is the case with missions further up, they had for a long time been used to the idea that missionaries were Europeans, and so my appearance as a local person did not bring out the idea of a missionary. On the other hand, I had a few colleagues who were convinced that the only way I did the work I did was because I was getting a huge salary, and not that I wanted to offer my services to the people. Despite these minor inconveniences, I soldiered on.

There are many settlement centres in North Horr that came about because of the church. Wherever the missionaries went, a nursery school was the first thing they established. Later, they started slowly catechising the children as well as the parents that were willing to attend. Soon there was a small church building, and then, of course, the snow-ball effect that would lead to a bigger population of people and settlements. In North Horr, I witnessed the growth of such a centre right next to my school that in two years grew into an Out- Station. Some of these have grown to be recognised as administrative centres where the government has set up Health Clinics and gone ahead to build primary schools. The growth of these centres has ensured the people some relative security since the police are often deployed there. North Horr itself has become a booming centre of commerce, and a political hub of sorts. There is the presence of International Non-Governmental Organizations (NGOs) that do their bit to improve the lives of the people. The church has always remained the central and focal point in these centres, often referred to as "the Vatican" of this or that place.

The Role of the Church

Owing to the obvious marginalization by the state government, a gap has been left in the North of Kenya, that the church has then been forced to fill. I witnessed in North Horr, people walk past, and even sometimes through, the Police Station to come to report to the priest an obvious police issue. People have grown accustomed to the fact that the police who are sent to work there would rather be elsewhere. The North isn't the first choice for any policeman, and for the "unfortunate" ones who find themselves there, it isn't "business as usual." The lethargy with which they respond to people's cries is a testimony of their morale. They, just like most people from "down country," come in with their stereotypes of the Northerners that don't help matters any.

I visited Illeret and was surprised at the number of underage mothers. Most of these children will never get to know their fathers. This is because every so often a battalion of the Paramilitary Unit, the General Service Unit (GSU), comes along and once their tour of duty is over, leave behind these pregnant girls, meaning that poverty levels go a notch higher, not to mention the spread of STDs including as HIV. There surely is no place for these girls to turn to other than the Mission, where the Benedictines have set up a clinic.

There was trouble once at a place called Gus, again an Out-Station of North Horr, where warriors from a neighbouring community attacked the people. When help came, albeit too late, the officers ended up ransacking the people's property and made away with cash which the people are forced to hide in their houses as no banks are found within their reach. Were it not for the intervention of the priests, it would have been double tragedy for the people, as they already had lost their livestock.

The first time I attended Mass at North Horr something happened that left my mouth ajar. The priest, just after consecration, brought to the front a special Chalice containing the Body of Christ and presented it to the people. Anyone from the old to the young, women and men solemnly walked to the altar and placed their hands on it. That act in itself was so significant to some of the people it was as much as receiving the Eucharist. I was baffled and scandalised for sure. I had never witnessed such an act before. I grew up with a great reverence for everything on the Altar, so naturally this act was unsettling to me.

Among the Gabbra people, they have a ritual sacrifice called *Soorio* that is the highest form or religious expression. The sacrificial lamb is one without blemish and only the clean people are allowed to attend. During the ceremony, people go and ritually touch the lamb. Not everyone, though, gets that honour. There are those that are ritually unclean – the adulterous, murderers, etc.– who are not allowed to do so.

In Christianity, Christ is that sacrificial Lamb of God, who takes away the sin and guilt of the "unclean." The early missionaries had been able to integrate Christianity and this very important aspect of the Gabbra culture quite flawlessly; it all made sense to the people. Later I would sit at Mass and marvel as I watched the smiles on the faces of those that were able to touch the Lamb of God, Jesus really. And here it did not matter what your past was: if you had made things right with God, you were good to go. One day I just stood up, I was a Gabbra, I was Christian, and I just went and touched Jesus!

Among the Gabbra, once it was discovered a girl was pregnant before marriage. She was ostracised; her fate left to the unknown. Some lucky ones got married to neighbouring communities, but that never changed their status in their own community. In North Horr centre, such unfortunate girls are present. The difference with the past is that the Christian community has embraced them. The priests have taken some of them for vocational training. This surely is what Christianity is about: Jesus came to give us a second chance. Who are we to shun those who have stumbled and are asking for a second chance?

The girl child in Kenya doesn't get much opportunity. You can imagine then how it is in the North. Bishop Cavallera Girls' School at Karare, Marsabit, was not there in the years I was in North Horr. I have, however, had numerous opportunities to visit the school, where we have several CLMs working with the Consolata Sisters. They are giving girls from the North a great opportunity to make the most of their God given potential. Would you believe, in their very first attempt at the National secondary level examination, the Kenya Certificate of Secondary Education (KCSE), they were top in the District? They have consistently since then managed to keep the same position and send girls to University. Last year was no disappointment; in fact, they were among the top 100 schools in the country. I can predict today that surely the day is coming when a woman will hold a special position in the communities around Marsabit and, I can bet, she will most likely have come through Bishop Cavallera Girls' School.

Among the communities in North Horr, they was an obvious hierarchy of importance, with some groups being looked down upon. It was so obvious that some people even lived in a small *manyatta*, separate from the rest of the community. Yet, what was so of the community special was that amongst the Christian community, such boundaries were quashed. We had the senior Catchiest come from one of the smaller clans, and everyone looked at him with respect. A second one came from a tribe that was perceived as illiterate. His brilliance was always evident whenever we met in the Parish pastoral planning meeting. There was a senior mechanic, who came from one of the "enemy" tribes. His community and the Gabbra clashed several times during my stay, yet no one seemed bothered by his presence.

Christianity is slowly but surely reaching to the corners of these communities, and I am hopeful that the stronger the faith gets the weaker the barriers that separate people will get. Are we there yet? No. Are we getting there? Definitely.

God Among the Marginalized

"What good can come out of Nazareth?" they asked. I was a young Christian when I went to North Horr and, of course, I thought much highly about myself then. Remember, here I was, feeling called to go and serve the marginalized. And so, I must admit I did do a lot of growing up, and I came to learn that up North the Spirit of God is as much present as anywhere in the world. I learnt that simply because people are marginalized does not at all imply they have an inferior culture, understanding, intelligence, or are out of touch with their needs and aspirations. For sure they would be needy as a direct result of being denied their fundamental rights, but the people surely are human just as we are.

We were on our way to Dukana, an Out-Station, when one of the priests suggested we take a detour and visit his friend. The friend is an old man who was among the first converts to Christianity in the region. What struck me was his faith. Here was this *"mzee"* (elder), who actually had one-on-one conversations with God. He communicated his desires to God and occasionally got into arguments – strong ones – with God! He spoke to God as a one would to a friend. I was "armed" and ready to preach the Good News to this man, yet my idea of God was this menacing, stick wielding God that was ready to pounce on me when I went astray! The *mzee* surely had found the Good News. We sat there for hours listening to him, the priest and myself.

There was also Maria Gorretti. We all refereed to her as the catchiest-at-large. She did not have any formal education, never attended Catechetical School, and yet was always at the right place at the right time to help people through difficult times. I asked her once how she decided to go to a place and she told me it was the Holy Spirit that sends her. And true to Jesus' command, Maria never drew a salary from any of the parishes she would transverse; nor did she seek boarding whenever she went. She just came, was accommodated by the Christians, did her good work, and left for her next assignment, led by the Holy Spirit

These experiences taught me that there is need for mutuality when it comes to Christians moving into the marginalized areas. A lot of good does exist there; we just need to be open to the fact that as good intentioned as we may be, we need to be ready and receptive of the good that is there. I grew in my faith in the North, and, yes, so much good did came from Nazareth.

Throughout the world, one thing the marginalized populations have in common is that they are denied their basic human rights. It used to take us then – it still does today – a good day and a half, sometimes even longer, to travel the less that 100 kilometres from Marsabit to North Horr. It was a nightmare trying to travel to Illeret.

Hopeful Signs

One of the direct consequences of marginalized people receiving the gospel is that they then wake up and fight against their marginalization. People in Moyale and Marsabit Diocese got tired of the poor roads and organised a demonstration. Under the auspices of the Catholic Justice and Peace Commission (CJPC), they organised the Great North Trek. They walked from Moyale to Isiolo and along the way were met by senior government officials, including the then Minister for roads. Today, the greatest part of the road from Isiolo towards Marsabit has been fixed whilst work on that from Moyale towards Marsabit has begun. The truth is that some selfish people, particularly the elite, do realise that the road means not only opening the region to the rest of Kenya, but also that the people will have their eyes open to what they have been denied. The church facilitated the walk because Christianity is about living your life to the full extent that God desires for us.

As I have previously mentioned. I taught in a public school.

What was strange was that the church was in-charge of the financial management of the school. For a period of time, the school had been mismanaged and was on the verge of collapse when the government appointed a new head and left the financial management to the Parish Priest of North Horr.

"Education is the key to the future" may be an over used cliché, but it still remains very relevant to the marginalized communities. While in North Horr, I taught from Monday to Thursday and spent my weekends visiting the numerous primary schools that the parish had in each settlement. It is of interest to note that *Mzee* Kimani Maruge, at one time the oldest primary school student in the world, said he joined school at his age to be able to read the Bible.

I know we gave our learners an opportunity to be something more in their lives. In my own small way, I know I helped free my former students from the yoke of not knowing what lies beyond their familiar territory. With the assistance of the Parish Priest and my colleagues, we organised a school tour and brought some boys to Nairobi. For some, that may as well have been the last time they would come over this way. For the majority, I know it lit in them a burning desire to venture out and discover more. It is of interest that the local MP then, the late Dr. Bonaya Godana, himself an educational beneficiary of the church, went out of his way to facilitate the boys' stay in Nairobi.

I meet great people who owe their education to the early missionaries and it is evident a seed was planted in them. When I was still in North Horr, these educational beneficiaries of the church had formed an "old boys association" which, as we speak, has opened a new boarding primary school for girls as well as a secondary school. One day, I know, both boys and girls in North Horr will have good access to education. When that time comes, it wont really matter how it all begun. A bright future will be in the offing and that's all that will matter.

I know for a fact that a people's health and security ought to be a top priority of any government, yet, as already mentioned, very little seems to be done on either front.

I once visited a place in North Horr where the government appointed nurse officially resided in Marsabit town, a day's journey from North Horr. I thought that was the height of madness! In contrast back at the

Mission, there was always someone on stand-by at the radio at designated times, and a driver at the ready in case of a medical emergency. People could be evacuated from far flung parts of the parish, some even air lifted to Mt. Kulal or Nairobi.

At Illeret, I once joined a Benedictine Brother, who is a medic, on his rounds. Most of the people he attended to had no idea of who he was or what Christianity was all about, but that did not deter him. He simply loaded his car with medicine, took along a guide and translator, and went on his way to help people in need. In one village, we found an old woman who was very ill. He tried his best to help but she passed on. It was sad, for sure, but I do know the woman died in dignity. I should mention that she had been left for dead when her kin noticed she was too sick.

My house was right next to the dispensary and that allowed me the opportunity to see just how important the place was. There was almost not a single night that ailing people didn't come along to wake up the nurse. Some would have travelled for days, and you should have seen their desperate looks. I always asked myself, "What if this mission was not here?" You actually shudder at that prospect.

Many years after I left North Horr, a Consolata priest, Fr Tony Bellagamba, talked to us about "Models of Mission." He mentioned "Radical Discipleship" as one. This took me back to some special people I encountered up North. There was this Africa Inland Church (AIC) missionary couple at Illeret, who lived for many years there. They had a young family, and they chose to bring up their kids there. I remember seeing these two kids running in the village barefoot with the other kids, playing and rolling in the dirt with no care in the world. I am not 100% sure, but I don't think the couple had set up huge social projects, I know they didn't even have an elaborate church building. Yet there they were, having chosen to live as committed Christian models among the Dasenech.

Back home at our mission, there was Madam Hildergarde, as everyone fondly called her. In her early years, she was most active in many aspects of the growth and development of the parish and, I dare say, the diocese. However, in her sunset years, with age and deteriorating health, she couldn't really do much. When it was obviously time for her to go back, Madam chose to stay amongst the people she loved, the Gabbra. Just the fact that she stayed was a real testimony of her love for the people. People enjoyed coming over and chatting with her before and after Mass, and you could see she enjoyed it too. Personally, she was a great inspiration. Madame passed on a year after I left, and was buried in North Horr. She had lived in the desert all these years; why couldn't I stay a couple of years? On the other hand, I do miss the lovely Sunday meals she prepared, as we all had a meal together once a week. The Lasagne and Pizza!

Negative Experiences Too

I also wish to state that some things did happen that were not at all great, and I feel our presence there as missionaries contributed to this. I remember once I was walking towards the priests' house and there was this huge crowd milling around. On enquiry, I was told that these were poor people who came for financial assistance. Well and good, for among the people I did see the very old and disabled who obviously needed assistance. However, among these were able bodied people. It was easier for the latter group to beg for alms rather than ask for gainful employment. Such a culture, I noticed, was not only in North Horr but in most places where there happens to be missionaries. We so much want to help that sometimes we cross the boundary and create unnecessary dependency.

I also learnt the hard way that there are two cadres of "poor" people. When I landed in North Horr, several people came over to me and were more than willing to preach their poverty to me. They had the saddest stories, with expressions and emotions to match. These are people who capitalise on the naivety of a new missionary for their own selfish ends. Of course, later I realised that these people were not at all poor; this was just a way of survival they had developed and mastered. But there were then the genuine poor. Some lived a stone's throw away from me at a *manyatta* sadly called *"Manyatta TB."* Throughout the years that I lived next to them, not a single day did anyone come over to ask for anything. At some point I thought it wise to go over and make friends. I was shattered at their level of poverty, yet not a single day did they come to me for charity. I learnt I should be very careful with the use of the term "poor" as for some people it is an insult to their position in life since they are at a low place in their lives and are struggling to get out, while for others it is a means to an end. People throw the word around for whoever was willing to listen.

I sometimes had a feeling that we did condone behaviour and practices that were obviously wrong, just so to keep the peace. We were in Gabbra territory, yes, but the fact remains that people from different communities did indeed call North Horr home. It was not so obvious, but I realised there was discrimination, and this was due to the fact was that there were people who acted as "gatekeepers" and controlled who got what. Silent as it was, it existed. The height of this was when once bales of cooking flour were destroyed because they had expired. Just how did this happen in a place where people constantly go to bed hungry, where children suffer malnutrition? But it did happen. Well, someone was stingy enough not to feed the entire group of needy people and only concentrated on his kinfolk, who obviously couldn't finish the entire food supply.

One time we went for *Jumuiya* or Small Christian Community meeting. It was lovely, and we were even served tea afterwards. On our way back I noticed that many people from the mission were rather quiet. I then was told that the stools we sat on and the table we were served tea on had actually come from the mission workshop. We were absolutely sure they had never been paid for. We knew something fishy was going on, but what to do? We chose not to upset the apple cart. Much as something was obviously wrong, the greater good work was in progress, and so again, what to do?

As most African cultures, there are obviously some practices here that go against what Christianity stands for. The Gabbra culture is no exception. There is female genital mutilation, for example. Much as we spoke against it and had seminars about it still went on. There are Christians that took part in it, and the big question was, what do we do? There were also early marriages; young girls were married off at an age when they needed to be in school and it was done even by Christians. Not only do the men have multiple partners, even the married women have men on the side. We at the mission knew this was going on and didn't feel capable of addressing the issue.

Conclusion

I had a wonderful time as a missionary in the north and I always look forward to the visits we make to the CLMs who are in the field. Despite the challenges we encounter we still are strong and able to move on. The knowledge that what we do matters and that it makes a difference in the lives of the people we are sent to is motivation enough.

Mr. Felix Ngao is a member of Catholic Lay Missionaries. He is in charge of administration. He has worked in various parts of the country and especially among the marginalized communities in Eastern province in areas such as Marsabit, North Horr among others.

Break-out Discussion Group Report on Evangelization in the Marginalized Communities in Northern Kenya

Mr. Francis Kimani

• There is a language barrier: some can hardly speak Swahili.
• There are numerous social issues, e.g. many young mothers and multiple sexual partners.
• The CLM did not speak out as much against the evils in the communities, e.g., early marriages and polygamy, because these are highly rooted traditions and speaking against them would have led to conflict.
• There are IDPs there since 2005.
• There are untold cases of people dying of hunger and other ailments.
• There is unhealthy competition from NGOs and CBOs. They use the people to get money from donors and the government, but this never gets to the intended people. More collaboration with stakeholders needed.
• Corruption is a great hindrance to development in the region. Most public services that should be given freely are sold at exorbitant prices.
• Marginalized areas are used as dumpsites. The US army has been accused of dumping dangerous chemicals in the ground that has led to increased diseases, including cancer.
• There is need to use the local communities to reach to these needy people.

- There is the problem of people committing themselves for the required two years period but later pulling out when the opportunity they were awaiting for elsewhere comes along.

Lay people have much to contribute – as, for example, the Kenyatta University's Catholic Community Missionary Outreach program which gives students a chance to reach out to the less fortunate in the society for usually between three to twelve weeks.

Theology of Mission

Rev. Patrick Mwania Musau, CSSp

The Theological Foundation of Mission *"ad Gentes"*

The word "Mission" in its common usage is ambiguous and therefore not easy to define. Etymologically, the word comes from the Latin verb *mittere* (an act of being sent) and in it twofold realities are expressed: First, the sending of a person by he who has the powers to send and, secondly, a specific task that the sender entrusts to the person sent. As such, mission expresses the nature of the task entrusted by the sender to the person sent, the aim of the mission itself and the receiver of mission.[1] In an attempt to capture the all-embracing definition of Mission, one can say that it is the task of announcing the Gospel of Christ to the people of all nations by making them into disciples of Christ, calling them to repentance and faith, in accordance to Christ's command: "Go therefore and make disciples of all the nations, baptizing them in the name of the Father and of the Son and of the Holy Spirit, teaching them to observe all things that I have commanded you..." (Matt 28:19-20). Christian Mission is the act of proclaiming, serving, and witnessing to God's reign of love, salvation and justice.

Often, Mission is used as a synonym of *evangelization* in its broader sense to sum up the Church's entire calling. One of the Vatican II Documents cautions against narrowing the term evangelization to explicit verbal proclamation only and stresses its broader sense: "In

---

1   Cf. Giuseppe Buono, *Missiology: Theology and Praxis* (Nairobi: Paulines Publications Africa, 2002), 55-58.

any case, to evangelize does not mean simply to teach a doctrine, but to proclaim Jesus Christ by one's words and actions, that is, to make oneself an instrument of his presence and action in the world."[2] According to Paul VI, evangelization is

Carrying forth of the Good News to every sector of the human race so that by its strength it may enter into the hearts of men and renew the human race… In a word, the Church may be truly said to evangelize when, solely in virtue of that news which she proclaims, she seeks to convert both the individual consciences of men and their collective consciences, all the activities in which they are engaged and finally, their lives and the whole environment which surrounds them. [3]

Mission *Ad Gentes* on the other hand means literally "Mission to the nations" and it is used as a Mission theological model to refer to the Church's unceasing responsibility of communicating the Gospel to those people who have scarcely or not yet heard at all about Jesus Christ. The Encyclical Letter *Redemptoris Missio* of John Paul II defines Mission Ad Gentes as the Church's activity of "proclaiming Christ and his Gospel, building the Local Church and promoting the values of the Kingdom," an activity which is directed to "peoples, groups and socio-cultural contexts in which Christ and His Gospel are not known, or which lack Christian communities sufficiently mature to be able to incarnate the faith in their own environment and proclaim it to other groups".[4]

Theologically, Mission or evangelization in the sense of proclaiming the Good News of salvation to all people takes three major dimensions as it is succinctly treated by John Paul II in *Redemptoris Missio*. He distinguishes clearly these three basic components of missionary activity in the world today. First and foremost, the Pontiff talks of Mission as *Mission ad Gentes,* sometimes called "primary evangelization". This refers to the missionary activity directed to "peoples or groups who do not yet believe in the Gospel," those "who are far from Christ," those in whom the Church "has not taken root" and whose culture has not

---

2   Vatican II, *Doctrinal Notes on Some Aspects of Evangelization*, No. 2.

3   Paul VI, Post-Synodal Exhortation *Evangelii Nuntiandi*, No. 18.

4   John Paul II, Encyclical Letter *Redemptoris Missio*, No. 33.

yet been influenced by the Gospel.[5]

The second category of the missionary activity of the Church falls under the pastoral activity which the Church undertakes among her faithful members. This is a kind of mission directed to Christian communities which have been already established and have adequate and solid ecclesial structures and are fervent in their faith and in Christian living. As already established ecclesial groups, they bear witness to the Gospel in their surroundings and have a sense of commitment to the universal mission.[6]

Finally, there is another dimension of the missionary activity of the Church known as re-evangelization or new evangelization. This is a kind of evangelizing activiyy which is undertaken by the Church to respond to a reality which particularly in countries with ancient Christian roots, and occasionally in the younger churches as well, entire groups of the baptized have lost a living sense of faith, or even no longer consider themselves members of the Church, and live a life far removed from Christ and his Gospel.[7] In such a situation, the Church sees her role in re-evangelizing to mean re-rooting the Good News of Christ and the Gospel values in the lives of people.

I would like now to focus on the first category of the missionary activity of the Church today which is *Mission ad Gentes,* as it forms the major area of interest in this presentation. Mission *ad Gentes* as a form of mission has been a point of controversial discussion among theologians in recent years. This came about due to the paradigm shift brought about by Vatican II in the way the world outside the Church and particularly non-Christian religions are to be viewed in relation to the economy of salvation in Jesus Christ. Vatican II is regarded as a watershed in the modern Christian theology of other faiths for it recognizes the presence of the Spirit in other religions, the admirable positive and precious elements, both religious and human which are true and good and which the Spirit qualifies to be regarded as "preparation for the Gospel", a gift from him who enlightens all human beings that

---

5 *Cf.* John Paul II, Encyclical Letter *Redemptoris Missio*, No. 34.

6 *Cf.* John Paul II, Encyclical Letter *Redemptoris Missio*, No. 33.

7 *Cf.* John Paul II, Encyclical Letter *Redemptoris Missio*, No. 33.

they may finally have life.[8]

The Catholic Church rejects nothing holy in these religions. She has a high regard for the manner of life and conduct, the precepts and teachings, which, though differing in many ways from her teaching, nonetheless often reflects a ray of that truth which enlightens all men.[9]

The Council sees the role of the Church in this regard to consist in trying in a spirit of openness and authenticity to strive to accent what is shared and valued in common and not what brings division. She should "prudently and lovingly, through dialogue and collaboration with the followers of other religions, and in witness to the Christian faith and life, acknowledge, preserve, and promote the spiritual and moral good as well as the socio-cultural values found among them.

This pronouncement of the Vatican II that there are elements of truth in other religions and that adherents of other religions could experience salvation has a lot of implications on the theology and praxis of Mission. A relevant question among some scholars in this regard has been about the validity and justification of *Mission ad Gentes*. Is mission to non-Christians and particularly among adherents of other religious traditions still necessary and if so, what form does it take. What should be the basic motivation and goal of mission to the nations, if non-Christian religions may be regarded as playing a significant role in the salvation of their followers? These questions among others become for mission theology and missionary congregations and societies, specifically founded for the evangelisation of non-Christians not merely of academic interest but of intrinsic value because they touch upon the very *raison d'être* of the Church's existence and nature which is fundamentally Mission.

Vatican Council II which is said to have brought about the watershed in the Catholic mission teaching by developing a more dynamic understanding of the missionary responsibility of the Church both within and without its own ecclesial boundaries was very clear on the continual validity of the Church's mission to non-Christians.

---

8   *Cf.* Vatican Council II, Constitution *Lumen Gentium*, No. 16.

9   Vatican Council II, Decree *Nostra Aetate*, No. 1.

The Council, despite the recognition that in ways better known to God Himself there is salvation for those living outside the Church, affirms the need of proclaiming the Good News of salvation especially to the people of other faiths, through the Church. It pointed out that the Church cannot compromise explicit proclamation of the Gospel to all people which is her identity and mission.

Although in ways known to himself God can lead those, who through no faults of their own, are ignorant of the Gospel, to that faith without which it is impossible to please him (Cf. Heb 11:6), the Church still has the obligation and also the sacred duty to evangelize all men.[10]

The need for the missionary Church to participate in the quest for truth cannot be disregarded even in the name of a legitimate religious pluralism. At the beginning of its Declaration on Religious Freedom, Vatican II says:

All are bound to seek the truth, especially in what concerns God and his church and to embrace the truth they come to know, and hold fast to it... It is in accordance with their dignity as persons... that all should be at once impelled by nature and also bound by moral obligation to seek the truth, especially religious truth. They are also bound to adhere to the truth, once it is known, and to order their whole lives in accord with the demands of the truth... Truth, however, is to be sought after in a manner proper to the dignity of the human person and his social nature. The inquiry is to be free.

The point which Vatican II is making here is that there is a continual necessity, relevance and urgency of the Church's *Mission ad Gentes* and that this Mission must include the explicit proclamation of Christ as saviour of the world. Salvation that is not only interior, personal and spiritual and other worldly reality but rather an integral reality embracing the material and spiritual, the personal and political-historical aspects of human existence[11] is offered to everyone, but never apart from the mediation of Christ and his Church, which is "the sacrament of

---

10 Vatican Council II, Decree *Ad Gentes*, No. 7.

11 *Cf.* John Paul II, Encyclical Letter *Redemptoris Missio*, No. 11.

salvation for all mankind". While there is no salvation outside Christ,[12] the Church is a necessary visible and tangible mediation which God uses as instrument in carrying out his plan of salvation. This realization brings us to some fundamental mission theological considerations as will be discussed here below.

The Church is by Nature and Essence Missionary

Vatican Council II defined the Church as missionary by nature by declaring evangelization to be fundamental to the Church's being and identity.

The Church on earth is by its very nature missionary, since according to the plan of the Father, it has its origin in the mission of the Son and the Holy Spirit. This plan flows from 'fountain-like love', the love of God the Father.

This radical statement of Vatican II emphasizes a number of theological implications. At the heart, or better core, of the Church's existence, indeed essentially and fundamentally to her missionary vocation, is the Trinity rooted and centred evangelization of the world and society in the sense of the "proclamation of the Gospel" (Mt 16:15) to "all nations" (Mt 28:19) "up to the earth's remotest end" (Acts 1:8). Accordingly the Church's reason for existence becomes the missionary sending, the commission, so that mission cannot only be a subsidiary, additional or secondary task of the Church, but indeed its major pre-occupation.

Theologically therefore, Church and mission are complimentary, two sides of the same coin. The Church cannot exist without Mission; she exists by way of evangelizing, indeed she exists in order to evangelize. Mission is the origin, the meaning and the final goal of the Church's existence. Indeed "it is plain that missionary activity wells up from the Church's inner nature and spreads abroad her saving Faith"[13] As a consequence, the Church fulfils and realizes her very nature by realizing her mission.

Mission of the Church is founded in the Blessed Trinity

---

12 „For there is only one God, and there is only one mediator between God and humanity, himself a human being, Christ Jesus, who offered himself as a ransom for all" (1 Tim 2:5-6).

13 Vatican Council II, Missionary Declaration, *Ad Gentes*, No. 6.

Ad Gentes 2 presents "Mission" of the Church as an image and a consequence of Christ's Mission and that of the Holy Spirit according to the decree of God the Father. The Mission of the Church locates its origin in the Mission of the Father, the mission of the Son and the Mission of the Holy Spirit. It is in the Mission of the blessed Trinity that the Mission of the Church is founded; it depends upon it and in it it finds its source and power. Mission has thus not only a Trinitarian character but an eschatological dimension as well for its owes its origin and realization to the mystery of the three persons of the Trinity. As Irenaeus puts it, it is in the trinity that mission finds its origin, essence, purpose and destiny.

The Holy Spirit and Jesus are two hands of God at work in the world. There is one Mission, the Mission of the Trinity, in which the Mission of the Spirit has a spatial and chronological priority over the mission of Jesus of Nazareth. God is two-handed so to speak, not one-handed.[14]

Christ's missionary commission "as the Father has sent me, so I am sending you," articulated in the Gospel of John[15] can be regarded as the point of departure of the Trinitarian understanding of the basis of Mission. The last mystery of Mission from which she exists, lives and grows is in fact the fact that God the Father sends the Son and the Father and the Son send the Holy Spirit. In this way, the God of the Trinity is not only simultaneously the one sending and the one being sent, but also the ultimate sending of self.[16]

Mission is basically a *Missio Dei* – a divine enterprise of God because He is Himself in essence a missionary God. Mission is an attribute of God because it is derived from the very nature of God who initiates any missionary project. God is the acting subject in any missionary enterprise and not the Church so that "the church can only follow in achieving what God has already done and is doing."[17] Consequently, mission cannot be an action of the Church

---

14 S. Smith, *The Holy Spirit in Mission*, p. 39.

15 *Cf.* Jn 20:21.

16 G. Vicedom, *The Mission of God*, 1960, p. 14.

17 G. F. Vicedom, *The Mission of God*, p. 6.

as such but first and foremost – indeed fundamentally an *actio Dei* (Act of God). It is God himself who initiates it and carries it out by sending Jesus Christ - who is the missionary par excellence – into the world through the Holy Spirit "who calls all humankind to Christ by the seeds of the word and by the preaching of the Gospel, stirs up in their hearts a submission to the faith."[18] The *missio Dei* in which the Church participates is accomplished by Christ who is sent by the Father to "gather together all the scattered children" so that all may be saved, certainly not "singly without any mutual visible bond" but by "moulding them into a people, God's people.[19]

Mission is fundamentally Christ centred – it has a strong Christological character as it finds its full realization and peak in the second person of the Trinity. Since Jesus is the subject and content of any authentic evangelization, any missionary proclamation cannot be genuine if it does not have Christ at its centre. According to John Paul II, "evangelization will always contain – as the foundation, centre and at the same time the summit of its dynamism – a clear proclamation that, in Jesus Christ... salvation is offered to all people, as a gift of God's grace and mercy."[20] Recalling the Fathers of the Second Vatican Council, Paul VI on a similar note asserts that Jesus "who Himself is the Good News of God" was from the very beginning (incarnation) to the end (crucifixion and resurrection) "the very first and the greatest evangelizer".[21] As a consequence, "there can be no true evangelization if the name, the teaching, the life, the promises, the kingdom and the mystery of Jesus of Nazareth the Son of God, are not proclaimed."[22]

If Christ is the subject and the content of any authentic proclamation, the Holy Spirit is the principal Agent of evangelization because it is the Holy Spirit who calls all humankind to Christ by the seeds of the word and by the preaching of the Gospel and who stirs up in their

---

18 Vatican Council II, Decree *Ad Gentes*, No. 15.

19 Cf. Vatican Council II, Decree *Ad Gentes*, No. 2.

20 John Paul II, Encyclical Letter *Redemptoris Missio*, No. 44.

21 Paul VI, Apostolic Exhortation *Evangelii Nuntiandi*, No. 7.

22 Paul VI, *ibid.*, Nos. 22 and 27.

hearts a submission to the faith.[23] The Holy Spirit "who is not to be regarded as an alternative to Christ or thought to fill a sort of void which is sometimes suggested as existing between Christ and the Logos" is the one who communicates God's message of love to the Church, empowering the Church to bring everything to the divine goal, so much that without Him there would be no Mission possible.

At the climax of Jesus' messianic Mission, the Holy Spirit becomes present in the Paschal Mystery in all of his divine subjectivity: as the one who is now to continue the salvific work rooted in the sacrifice of the cross. Of course Jesus entrusts this work to human beings: to the apostles, to the Church. Nevertheless, in and through them the Holy Spirit remains the transcendent and principal agent for the accomplishment of this work in the human spirit and in the history of the world.[24]

The Spirit is the principal agent in the sense that he is the one who empowers people to evangelize – the one who "acts in every evangelizer" by "placing on his lips the words which he could not find himself" and at the same time the one who "predisposes the soul of the hearer (of the Gospel) to be open and receptive to the Good News and to the Kingdom being proclaimed".[25]

The Universality of the Holy Spirit

The Holy Spirit is present in the Church but also outside the Church in non-Christian cultures and religious traditions. He is universal and effectively active among all peoples of all ages, in a variety of cultures and numerous religious traditions. The Spirit is mysteriously present in the heart of every human being, each group of people and all cultures and traditions are bound to be touched by him. It is thus possible to believe that the Spirit, in a manner known to God, is able to offer every person, irrespective of origin, race, worldview or religious belief, the possibility of sharing in the Paschal Mystery.

---

23 Vatican Council II, Decree *Ad Gentes*, No. 15.

24 John Paul II, Encyclical Letter *Redemptoris Missio*, No. 28.

25 *Cf.* Paul VI, Apostolic Exhortation *Evangelii Nuntiandi*, No. 75.

Vatican Council II has been instrumental in recognizing other religions as containing positive elements, which though not perfect as such, could be regarded as serving as pedagogy toward the true God, or as a preparation for the Gospel. The reason behind this paradigm shift in attitude towards other religions and non-Christian cultures is the conviction that God is present in the world through His Spirit. According to her teaching especially after Vatican II, the Church holds and teaches that the Holy Spirit is universally present in the world - even in non-Christian traditions and cultures. Evident in these cultures and traditions are some of the positive elements which cannot be regarded as fruit of merely human initiative but rather of the Holy Spirit. These are those elements of truth and grace that are to be found among the nations which are to be described as a "sort of secret presence of God".[26]

As a consequence, the Spirit of God is in a way present in the world outside the Church. The Holy Spirit is present in the world outside the Church and He is one who does the work of sowing "the seed of the Word" even before the coming of the missionary. The work of the Church in this context is to treasure these "traces" of God's presence in the world cultures and religious traditions and to help in purifying and enlightening these values with the Gospel which acting as a principle does not destroy but "conserves, purifies, heals, ennobles and perfects" the rites and customs in cultures and non-Christian traditions.

By her activity whatever good is found sown in the minds and hearts of human beings, or in the rites and customs proper to various peoples, is not only saved from destruction, but is also healed, ennobled and brought to perfection, for the glory of God, the confusion of the devil, and the happiness of human persons...[27]

Dialogue as an integral Part of the Church's Evangelizing Mission

Mission *Ad Gentes* means that kind of mission activity which the Church directs to cultures and religious traditions of the world that have not been in touch with the Gospel. This aspect of mission is based on the recognition that God was and is somehow also present

---

26 *Cf.* Vatican Council II, Constitution *Lumen Gentium*, No. 16.

27 J. Dupuis, *Toward a Christian Theology of Religious Pluralism*, p. 162.

in other religions, non-Western cultures, and in the world and society in general. The mysterious and wonderful movement of God's spirit, like the wind, cannot be captured within Church walls or certain geographical territories.

Dialogue with non-Christian cultures and religions is a priority for a Church which is by nature and being missionary. The theological basis of dialogue is provided in the example of God himself who through the mystery of incarnation entered into dialogue with humanity and in Christ who in many occasions during his ministry on earth entered into dialogue with different people of different cultural and religious standing. Christians who are in word and deed followers of Christ are called to dialogue with people of other cultures and religious traditions so that they might "learn of the riches which a generous God has distributed among the nations."[28] They are called to live "in esteem and love for believers of other religions, 'share in their cultural and social life by various exchanges and enterprises of human living' and get to familiarity with their national and religious traditions."[29]

According to the teaching of the Catholic Church, one of the important tasks of every Christian is to enter into a genuine dialogue, built on a profound respect for the religious other and the practice of dialogue should be at the heart of the Church's Mission.

The Church has therefore this exhortation for the faithful: prudently and lovingly, through dialogue and collaboration with followers of other religions and in witness of Christian faith and life, acknowledge, preserve and promote the spiritual and moral goods found among these people as well as the values in their society and culture.[30]

Indeed at different levels and different times, there has always been an encounter between the Gospel and the cultures and traditions of the world. Throughout history Christianity has come into contact with other religions and cultures – a contact that resulted in Christianity influencing

28 Vatican Council II, Declaration *Nostra Aetate*, No. 2.

29 Vatican Council II, Decree *Ad Gentes*, No. 11.

30 Vatican Council II, Declaration *Nostra Aetate*, No. 2.

these religions and cultures as well as being influenced by them.[31] Evangelization is a sublime task of the Church, which is directed to specific individuals or groups in a particular cultural and social context and in a given space and time. Culture is an essential constituent of human existence. As E. Nunnenmacher clearly points out: culture "is an essential characteristic of human existence: where there are human beings, there is a culture, because the human being is naturally a cultural being..."[32] Human beings are cultural beings and live within a framework of set cultural traditions which influence their way of life and behaviour. A faith-contact with an individuals necessarily implies contact with their culture, which is what defines people's manner of existence. It follows therefore that, in order for the Gospel to penetrate deeply into people's hearts and minds, in order for it to have its desired effect and transforming power, *it must not be foreign to their culture;*[33] *it has to touch the heart of the context of their culture*; indeed it has to be *incarnated in it,* i.e. to take flesh into the integral[34]mainstream of peoples' lives. The Gospel must become relevant and influential in peoples' lives; it has to be "translated into the total context of its hearers' history and present experience of faith".[35]

As a matter of principle, the Gospel message cannot remain foreign or a stranger to the people with whom it lives; it "must put down its roots in cultural, social and human terrains".[36] It must take root; it must be reformulated into the very thought-pattern of the people.[37] *It must*

---

31   The dialogue between the Gospel and culture has been an issue throughout the rich history of Christianity. According to New Testament accounts, the Gospel came into contact with different people in different cultural milieux. We witness for example the translation of the Christian message from its Hebrew mother culture to Greek culture which is altogether different. All this was done to make the message touch people's lives where and as they are.

32   E. Nunnenmacher, „Culture," p. 94.

33   Paul VI emphasized this point when he pointed out that "the gap between Gospel and culture is undeniably the tragedy of our time" (Apostolic Exhortation *Evangelii Nuntiandi*, No. 20).

34   The Gospel is meant for the integral salvation of the person in question. The inculturation process should also address all the aspects of life in the light of the Gospel values, with the intention of purifying and transforming the quality of each person's life, the environment, the community and indeed, the whole society. (*Cf.* A. Hope and S. Timmel, *Training for Transformation: A Handbook for Community Workers*, p. 66).

35   K. Müller, *Mission Theology* , p. 153.

36   Paul VI, Apostolic Exhortation *Evangelii Nuntiandi*, No. 62.

37   *Cf.* Vatican II, Pastoral Constitution *Gaudium et Spes* No. 44 and 66; Decree *Ad Gentes* No. 22.

be integrated into people's life in such a way that it acquires a home in their culture, so that it can touch their entire life within their own social milieu. The work of evangelization is bound to be effective if at all the Christian faith is deeply rooted, if it touches people's lives in the context of their culture. The Good News must not be preached in a foreign language which people do not understand but should be translated into the symbols and language that people understand. As Paul VI rightly said:

Evangelization loses much of its force and effectiveness if it does not take into consideration the actual people to whom it is addressed, if it does not use their language, their signs, their symbols, if it does not answer the questions they ask, and if it does not have an impact on their concrete life.[38]

Christianity is only real and authentic *if it takes flesh in the culture of a people.* Christian faith is *authentic if it finds its roots in human cultures thereby transforming them into the values of the Kingdom.* A Church is local and real if it is "incarnate in a people, a Church indigenous and inculturated".[39] The process by which Christianity becomes people's way of life by integrating the Gospel message into their concrete life situations is technically referred to as "inculturation," which can be defined as

... the incarnation of Christian life and of the Christian message in a particular cultural context, in such a way that this experience not only finds expression through elements proper to the culture in question, but becomes a principle that animates, directs and unifies the culture, transforming and remarking it so as to bring about a 'new creation'.[40]

Beside dialogue with human cultures, dialogue between Christianity and Non-Christian religions is another equally important element of the evangelizing Mission of the Church, like proclamation. Dialogue means "all positive and constructive inter-religious relations with

---

38 Paul VI, Apostolic Exhortation *Evangelii Nuntiandi*, No. 63.

39 *Cf.* "Statement of the Federation of Asian Bishops' Conference First Plenary Assembly," p. 122.

40 M. Dhavamony, "The Christian Theology of Inculturation" in *Studia Missionalia*, Vol. 44 (1995), p.3. This article can also be found in S. Iniobong Udoidem, *Pope John Paul II on Inculturation: Theory and Practice*, p. 5.

individuals and communities of other faiths which are directed at mutual understanding and enrichment, in obedience to truth and respect for freedom. It includes both witness and exploration of respective religious convictions."[41]

Vatican II and the successive Church teachings have repeatedly affirmed that inter-religious dialogue is a duty for all Christians; it "is much more than a way of promoting mutual familiarity with, and enrichment by, other faiths; it is a part of the Church's mission to evangelize, an expression of her *Missio ad Gentes.*"[42]

Inter-religious dialogue is essential, indeed an integral element of the Church's evangelizing Mission. According to John Paul II, "[I]nter-religious dialogue is a part of Church's evangelising mission"[43] because "dialogue is a path towards the Kingdom of God."[44] The Church is obliged to enter into dialogue with the world in which it lives because she has a message to deliver, a communication to make.[45]Dialogue is not to be seen as a tactic by Christians to convert others to Christianity as it has often been misunderstood. As Pope John Paul II remarks: "Dialogue does not originate from tactical concerns of self-interest, but is an activity with its own guiding principles, requirements and dignity." [46]

Rather, dialogue should be seen as an effective way of discovering the Spirit which is at work within all individuals of various religions. Dialogue is a means of seeking truth and of sharing it with others. Its fruit is harmonious living in communion with one another and with God since "by dialogue we let God be present in our midst; for as we open ourselves in dialogue to one another, we also open ourselves to God."[47] When Christians live with people of other religions, dialogue receives a central function, for it brings about love and mutual respect as well as taking away or at least diminishing hatred and prejudices

---

41 *Dialogue and Proclamation*, No. 9.

42 John Paul II, Post-Synodal Exhortation *Ecclesia in Asia*, No. 31.

43 John Paul, Post-Synodal Exhortation *Ecclesia in Asia*, No. 55.

44 *Ibid.*, No. 57.

45 Paul VI, Encyclical Letter *Ecclesiam Suam*, No. 65.

46 *Ibid.*, No. 56.

47 *Ibid.*, p. 597.

among the followers of various religions. It promotes unity and friendship among Christians and followers of other religions.[48] The fruit of dialogue is "… union between people and union of people with God, who is the source and revealer of all truth and whose Spirit guides men in freedom only when they meet one another in all honesty and love."[49]

Inter-religious dialogue is founded on the theological truth that all human beings have the same origin, namely, the Supreme God, who, at the same time, is the single destiny towards which man strives. All human beings have the same redeemer, Jesus Christ. And finally, the Holy Spirit is present and operative in all human beings without exception. Dialogue is not merely anthropological in character but theological too. Just as God, by way of the incarnation, opted to enter into dialogue with humankind so that "all may be saved", the Church must take as its vocation entering into dialogue with the entire world; with other religions and ideologies, with other Christian churches and within itself. The Church is called to continue the dialogue of God, who right from creation until today has been in constant dialogue with humankind.

In a world which is pluralistic and where freedom of expression of faith reigns, *dialogue* as a uniting principle is important and, perhaps, inescapable. In a world where religion tends to be a divisive factor, dialogue as an authentic form of Christian witness is obligatory. Given the current situation, which is marked by religious pluralism and diversity, dialogue becomes a *conditio sine qua non* of Christian existence. If the Church has to be faithful to her call of encountering people of other religions who share the same ultimate spiritual pursuit in genuine respect, the quest for the Absolute, the quest for God, then she has to embrace the Spirit of dialogue which is an "attitude of respect and friendship which permeates all activities constituting the evangelising Mission of the Church."[50] Dialogue is demanded today more than ever, by the dynamic course of action which is changing the face of modern society - it is demanded by the pluralism of society and

---

48 *Cf.* John Paul II, Apostolic Exhortation *Christifideles Laici*, No. 30.

49 *Ibid.*

50 Pontifical Council for Inter-religious Dialogue, *Dialogue and Proclamation*, No. 9.

by the maturity man has reached in this day and age - be he religious or not. Secular education has enabled people to think and speak, and to conduct dialogue with dignity.[51] The Church must, therefore, proclaim its specific *kerygma* in a way that is distinct from that of earlier ages and it can only do so dialogically.

In the Vatican II documents, dialogue with other religions is seen as something natural, a special character of the Church's Mission. In order to respond to the needs of our age, Christians are invited to track the paths of the spirit through dialogue, a dialogue that is not aimed at conversion, although it is not opposed to it, but at promoting progress in movement towards God, for both parties greater openness to divine action, and to salvation. This is why the Fathers of the Second Vatican Council exhorted all the Catholic faithful, lay and clergy alike, to recognise the signs of the times and to take part in enhancing ecumenism and dialogue with the adherents of non-Christian traditions.[52] Each Catholic has a vocation to use his talents to struggle out of the self-centred *monologue* mindset into *dialogue* with others as they are, not as we want them to be. Christians are called to stress what they have in common with others rather than what divides them, since "the ties which unite the faithful are stronger than those which separate them; let there be unity in what is necessary, freedom in what is doubtful, and charity in everything."[53] Accordingly, to be Christian is to be a herald and a disciple, a pilgrim and an eschatological witness with and for others. Since the Church is itself a learning Church in collaboration with others, Christian mission should assume an attitude of love, of listening and of learning. As Christians journey together with others, they become enriched with others – they enrich others and are enriched by them, by their anthropological, metaphysical, ascetical, mystical, and ritual values.

According to Paul VI, a genuine dialogue has to be preceded by a genuine recognition and acceptance of the values in other religions and their relevance. That is why he began his encyclical *Ecclesiam*

---

51 *Cf.* Paul VI , Encyclical Letter *Ecclesiam Suam,* No. 78.
52 *Cf.* Vatican Council II, Decree *Unitatis Redintegratio*, No. 4.
53 *Ibid.*, No. 38.

Suam by appreciating and praising every religion as containing sparks of light within itself, which must neither be despised nor quenched, even though they are insufficient for giving clear vision. In one of his speeches on the Easter Sunday of 1964, the Pontiff further said that:

> *Every religion has within it rays of light which must neither be disdained nor extinguished, even if they are not sufficient to offer man the clarity of which he is in need, and are incapable of arriving at the miracle of the Christian light, which enables truth to coincide with life. Every religion raises us to the transcendence of Being ... Every religion is the dawn of Faith ...*[54]

Echoing the voice of his predecessor, John Paul II talks explicitly about the need for, and urgency of dialogue with people of other religious traditions of the world. His call to dialogue is based on his strong conviction that because "the Holy Spirit is active within and outside the visible Body of the Church" and "because all human beings are called to one divine destiny", all people have a possibility of being associated, in a way known to God, with the Paschal Mystery.[55] In *Redemptor Hominis* John Paul II relates the redemption of Christ to each and every person, without exception. He affirms that the human person - every person without exception- has been redeemed by Christ; because Christ is in a way united to every person. Even if the individual may not realize this fact, Christ "can through the Spirit offer man the light and the strength to measure up to his supreme destiny".[56]

An interesting fact that John Paul II especially emphasizes is the redemptive presence of Jesus Christ to the entire human family, to people everywhere, to every single human being in his or her own concrete historical situation. This is where he bases his theological argument for inter-religious dialogue. Dialogue, the Pope remarks, is not in opposition to the mission *ad gentes*; in fact, it has special links with that mission and is one of its expressions. To proclaim the good news of God's love in Jesus Christ to all humanity is the essential duty of the Church.[57] Indeed for him dialogue and proclamation are not

---

54 Paul VI, Easter Radio Message to the World March 29, 1964," p. 120.
55 *Cf.* John Paul II, Encyclical Letter *Redemptoris Missio*, No. 28.
56 *Ibid.*, No. 14.
57 *Ibid.*, No. 44.

alternative but complementary; they are equally authentic elements of the evangelizing Mission of the Church whose goal is to make the salvific action of God be felt all over in human history. For him, "[i] nter-religious dialogue at its deepest level is a dialogue of salvation, because it seeks to discover, clarify and understand better the signs of the age-long dialogue which God maintains with mankind."[58] As such an authentic dialogue, which is open and disinterested, objective and frank, one which excludes pretence, rivalry, deceit and betrayal[59] "leads to inner purification and conversion which, if pursued with docility to the Holy Spirit, will be spiritually fruitful".[60]

Indeed

The fruit of dialogue is union between people and union of people with God, who is the source and revealer of all truth and whose Spirit guides men in freedom only when they meet one another in all honesty and love. By dialogue, we let God be present in our midst, as far as we open ourselves in dialogue to one another, we also open ourselves to God.[61]

Church life today devoid of respectful recognition of other religions and mutual dialogue with them would be unimaginable and, in fact a grave sin of omission. Inter-religious dialogue is intrinsically necessary to the proclamation of the Gospel; it is a main constitutive aspect of faith in Jesus Christ and the Mission of the Church.

Conclusion: Proclaiming and Promoting the Reign of God as the Goal of all Mission

Proclamation and promotion of the Kingdom of God is the ultimate goal of mission and the Church's vocation is located in the context of this goal. The kingdom builds the *framework*, the *centre* and the *purpose* or *goal* of Jesus' message and mission and that of the Church as well.

---

58 John Paul II, "To the Plenary Session of the Pontifical Council of Inter-religious Dialogue, Rome, November 13th.1992," p. 498.

59 *Cf.* Paul VI, Encyclical Letter *Ecclesiam Suam*, No. 110.

60 John Paul II, Encyclical Letter *Redemptoris Missio*, No.56.

61 John Paul II, "To Representatives of the Various Religions of India, Madras, February 5, 1986," p. 326.

Indeed the fundamental task of mission is to proclaim and promote the kingdom of God. The mission of the Church is a continuation of the mission of Christ which was the inauguration of God's reign on earth. The Church is entrusted with "the mission of announcing and inaugurating [God's kingdom] among all peoples."[62]

Jesus the principal evangelizer, spent his life proclaiming the Good News of the Kingdom and the salvation integral to it. "… By words and deeds, by signs and miracles, and more especially by His resurrection and by sending of the Spirit of Truth,"[63] Jesus set out to bear witness to the kingdom. The central purpose of Christ's life was the proclamation and inauguration of the Kingdom of God. Jesus understands His entire Mission in the context of the proclamation of the Kingdom and He works as the servant for this kingdom till death. The kingdom was "not only the central theme in Jesus' preaching, the reference point of most of his parables and the subject of a large number of his sayings, it was also the content of his symbolic actions".[64]

The content of this reality, the kingdom, is the reign of freedom, fellowship and love. It is God's own order of truth, love, justice and peace. John Paul II describes the kingdom as the "communion among all human beings with one another and with God."[65] The kingdom of God has a transforming power, for it possesses a power that transforms human relationships enabling them to learn to love, forgive and serve, thus building a familial communion with one another and with God based on the law of love.[66] It is an order of integral liberation, encompassing human existence in all its dimensions, personal and communal, spiritual and material. It is an order that has a special preference for the poor. Jesus' ministry and message targeted all people, sinners and the just, Jews and Gentiles, the poor and the rich alike. Jesus brings the good news of the Kingdom particularly to the *anawim* of Yahweh, the poor and the marginalized, those in the periphery of the society. His word

---

62 John Paul II, Encyclical Letter *Redemptoris Missio*, No. 20.

63 Paul VI, Apostolic Exhortation *Evangelii Nuntiandi*, No. 12.

64 J. Fuellenbach, *The Kingdom of God: The Central Message of Jesus Today*, p. 43.

65 *Cf.* John Paul II, Encyclical Letter *Redemptoris Missio*, No. 15.

66 *Cf.* John Paul II, Encyclical Letter *Redemptoris Missio*, No. 14-15.

and action initiate the dynamic activity of God that aims at bringing total salvation among the marginalised and the outcast, the lowly, the despised and less privileged people. To borrow Bosch's words: "God's reign is not intended for those who regard themselves as VIP's, but for those on the margins: for those who suffer, for tax-collectors and sinners, for widows and children."[67]

Like Mission in general, *Mission ad Gentes* has the goal of explicitly promoting the reign of God among those who are far away from Christ, those who have not heard about the Good News of Christ. The Church which must define herself in relation to the kingdom is called to proclaim the Good News of the kingdom to all human beings and indeed the whole of creation, mission that is proper to her nature and vocation. However, the Church is not to be equated to the kingdom; she is instead "symbol and servant of the Kingdom". Her vocation as a symbol is to be a light to the nations, to give a clear witness to the values of the kingdom. As a servant on the other hand, the Church should be able to promote the reign of God in the world, discerning the signs of the times and collaborating with all those graced movements by which the Holy Spirit is bringing about the realization of the Kingdom in and for the world at large. This Mission of the Church as a servant of the Kingdom can be classified in three essential and inter-related dimensions: human promotion, inculturating the Gospel into various world cultures so that it can become relevant to the hearers, and finally, engagement in dialogue with adherents of other religious traditions.

Bibliographical Sources

Bosch, J. David, *Transforming Mission: Paradigm Shifts in Theology of Mission* (Maryknoll, New York: Orbis Books, 1991).

Flannery, Austin (ed.), *Vatican Council II: The Conciliar and Post Conciliar Documents, Vatican Collections*, Vol. 1, New Revised Edition (Northport, New York: Castello Publishing Company, 1984).

---

67 D. Bosch, *Transforming Mission*, p. 33.

Fuellenbach, John, *The Kingdom of God: The Message of Jesus Today* (Maryknoll, New York: Orbis Books, 1995).

John Paul II, Encyclical Letter *Redemptoris Missio on the Permanent Validity of the Church's Missionary Mandate* (Vatican City: Libreria EditriceVaticana, 1991).

Nunnenmacher, Eugen, "Culture" in: Karl Mueller *et al.* (eds.), *Dictionary of Mission: Theology, History, Perspectives* (Maryknoll, New York: Orbis Books, 1997) 94-101.

Paul VI, Apostolic Exhortation *Evangelii Nuntiandi* on Evangelization in the Modern World, (London: Catholic Truth Society, 1975)..

----------,Encyclical Letter *Ecclesiam Suam* on the Church, in: *AAS*, Vol. 55, 1964, pp. 609-659.

Pontifical Council for Interreligious Dialogue and Congregation for the Evangelization of Peoples, "Dialogue and Proclamation," in: James A. Scherer and Stephen B. Bevans, *New Directions in Mission & Evangelization I* (Maryknoll, New York: Orbis Books, 1991) 177-200.

Vicedom, George F., *The Mission of God: An Introduction to the Theology of Mission* (St. Louis, Missouri: Corncordia, 1965).

Rev. Dr. Patrick Mwania Musau, CSSp holds a STD (Doctorate Degree in Sacred Theology) with specialization in Mission Theology from the Philosophisch, Theologische Hochschule, SVD, St. Agustine, Germany. He is currently a lecturer at Tangaza College in the Department of Mission Theology.

Break-out discussion Group
on Mission "ad Gentes"

Report by Participants

Question: For the indigenous African, how do you see the mission challenge? Fr. Mwania responded in this way: Before the Second Vatican Council mission belonged to the Church, the Church had to carry it out. Various Congregations and Societies had territorial areas given to them in different areas of the world, in African countries, for example. But after the Second Vatican Council mission is God's affair and human beings are instruments in this "Missio Dei."

Personal Comments

I feel the Catholic Church today is trying to evangelize. But I see that many Catholics are going to the Protestants. And, yes, some Protestants are coming to our church too. But I ask myself: the youth, where are they heading?

Another said, it is a question of culture. Cultures are changing now very rapidly. Is there a University here in our area that offers Missiology at a degree level? Because I feel that in the face of this need, the questions we see, I think we as a church are not treating mission in a comprehensive way. We need to.

Yes, Mission *ad gentes* – new cultures bring new questions.

I think we need so many more people involved in the evangelization process. And 9 years training (like so many formation programs now) results in very few. We need a new paradigm or something new or different to meet the challenge.

I refer to the Charismatic Movement – and I start by saying we need to learn why Catholic people are going to the Protestant churches. And I think we are looking for some of what is there! The dancing, the singing, the emotion; Okay, some is overdone or maybe out of place, but something is there that we lost in our church when we lost much of the charismatic spirit we had a few years ago.

The Church in Africa (Kenya) is growing, it is true. But, we have not made the *leap* to incorporating our African people to be missioners. That impulse or spirit is not strong among us. And it was much stronger years ago in our villages, when our churches were beginning.

I have a question about mission from above and mission from below. We need to think more about this. I am thinking, the church's mission also has a human aspect, and is a sinful church. I refer to the anniversary (coming next week) of the Rwandan genocide, carried out to a large extent by Christians and many Catholics on Christians and on many Catholics. And it leaves me with a question: Is mission the end of or goal of the establishment of the local Church?

My question is this: Can we differentiate the preaching of Christ from the works we do? I refer to the humanitarian works of bringing and distributing food, clothes, medical care, and so on. So my question is: What are we bringing as we "go out" to evangelize? NGOs and Muslims too can and do also bring food, etc. Is this a waste of time?

Time ran out for the break-out session with lots of interest and questions and not so many answers as each person wanted to ask his/her question or raise a point. There was a lot of interaction.

Part III
THEOLOGICAL REFLECTIONS
Greetings

Rev. Joseph Healey, MM

Good afternoon! Welcome to this third and final session of our mission symposium. My name is Fr Joseph Healey, a Maryknoll Missionary. During these two days we have experienced an inductive process starting from our mission and pastoral experience. Rather than the usual keynote speakers and lecture format we began with Panel Presentations on "Mission to Justice" with Breakout Discussion Groups on the various topics yesterday afternoon and Panel Presentations on "Mission ad Gentes (to the Nations)" with Breakout Discussion Groups on the various topics this morning. We heard mission testimonies from the grassroots, from the local level in Africa followed by discussion and sharing in our small groups. Now we have a Panel Presentation of theological reflections on these themes and experiences of mission. We welcome three distinguished African theologians to share their insights and reflections with us. Karibuni.

Theological Reflections on the Future of Mission in Africa

Rev. Laurenti Magesa

Church historian Father John Baur compares the beginning of Christianity in Africa to "trickling stream in the desert." But "God's providence never let ... it dry up," he writes. The stream steadily grew with time to "become a great flood watering the whole continent."[1]

How, precisely, the initial trickle turned into a torrent in the course of these 2000 years or so is a question for historians like Baur himself to explore.[2] For theologians the charge is somewhat different. Theirs is a call to attempt – always guided by faith that seeks understanding – to explore how these waters might continue to nourish the life of faith in contemporary Africa as well as in the days ahead. In other words, the theologian must try to map the movement of God's Spirit in the church and, wherever and whenever possible, by reading the signs of the time, to indicate potential canals through which to channel theological and pastoral energy into ever more fruitful and fulfilling evangelical outcomes.

---

1   John Baur, *200 Years of Christianity in Africa: An African Church History*. 2nd Edition (Nairobi: Paulines Publications Africa, 2009), 16.

2   And he does so admirably in the volume just mentioned, where the images of stream and flood for the development of the Church in Africa appear.

The Catholic Foreign Mission Society of America (popularly known as Maryknoll[3]) has been part of these Christian waters in several parts of the world for one hundred years now. Like every disciple of Christ and every member of the Church, Maryknoll needs to pause once in a while for thought on various issues of concern. Like everyone else, Maryknoll must occasionally take time off to reflect specifically on its mission in the global and local situations that form the context of the wider Christian mission. Perhaps one of the best opportunities to do this is when the organization is celebrating a century of its existence. Here, therefore, let us attempt to look at the future shape of the mission in which Maryknoll has formed a part for the last one hundred years and in which it will continue to be engaged in response to its calling by God.

Maryknoll in Africa

For the sake of better understanding and general benefit, we might as well begin with a note of historical interest about Maryknoll as an organization.[4] Similar to the commission of Jesus himself to his first disciples, Maryknoll's task was to be, as the commissioning bishops put it, "to recruit, send and support U.S. missioners in areas around the world."[5] Accordingly, beginning with East Asia, Maryknollers went to South America and, subsequently, Africa.

The pioneer Maryknoll priests arrived in Africa in the Lake region of northeastern Tanganyika (now Tanzania), at Nyakatende-Nyegina

---

3   "Maryknoll is a name shared by three organizations that are part of the Roman Catholic Church and whose joint focus is on the overseas mission activity of the Catholic Church in the United States. These organizations consist of two religious ordeers and one lay group: The Maryknoll Fathers and Brothers (The Catholic Foreign Mission Society of America); The Maryknoll Sisters (TheMaryknoll Sisters of St. Dominic); and the The Maryknoll lay Missioners. While sharing a name and similar origins, the organizations are independent entities that work closely together in many of their missionary endeavors." See "Maryknoll," http://en.wilkipedia.org/wiki/Maryknoll.

4   For this see also, Michael C. Kirwen, "Introducing the Symposium," at the beginning of this volume.

5   "Maryknoll," http://en.wilkipedia.org/wiki/Maryknoll. See Mt. 28:19-20.

in Musoma, in 1946.[6] During the century of Maryknoll's existence as a Catholic missionary society, and more than half a century of its presence in Africa, much has happened to influence it in many ways. This is reason enough to stop and take stock of its missionary vision so as to chart out what may be for it as a missionary society and for the church in general a more relevant course of action for the future.

In his encyclical letter, *Redemptoris Missio (The Mission of the Redeemer)*, Pope John Paul II calls upon the whole Church to do the same. The Pope explains this obligation with reference to the contemporary changed global conditions: "The rapid and profound transformations which characterize today's world," he says, "are having a powerful effect on the overall missionary picture." In concrete terms, the Pope notes that "Where before there were stable human and social situations, today everything is in flux. One thinks, for example, of urbanization and the massive growth of cities, especially where demographic pressure is greatest. In not a few countries, over half the population already lives in a few 'megalopolises,' where human problems are often aggravated by the feeling of anonymity experienced by masses of people" (no. 37).

On the one hand, there is the dominance of an exploitative global economy and the numerical expansion of the poor. On the other, there is an increasing awareness and commitment to peace, development and human rights in the world. These are some of the transformations that Pope John Paul II suggests should not be overlooked when thinking about "the future of mission." There is also, of course, the preponderance of the young in the overall global demographical picture, making the perception of the world and human expectations radically different than was the case only a few decades ago.[7]

All of this has to be brought into the scene when contemplating the future of mission locally and globally. We might refer to this whole

---

6   See "The Buffaloes: A Story of Maryknoll Society's Fifty Years in Tanzania," http://www. Maryknollafrica/Documents/Buffaloes.txt.
     "Maryknoll began its missionary work in Tanganyika, East Africa with the arrival of Fathers William Collins, Albert Good, Joseph Brannigan and Louis Bayless in Nyegina Mission in 1946. They were welcomed by the Missionaries of Africa (formerly called the White Fathers) under whose tutelage they would learn the tribal languages and culture. Each week the priests spent 2 to 3 days visiting the people in their homes." See http://www.maryknollafrica.org/tanzania.html.

7   See elsewhere in this volume, Philomena Njeri Mwaura, "The Quest for Holistic Mission in Africa."

exercise as "historical revisioning," a process that involves the attempt to bring to active collective memory those elements of mission that may have been inadvertently lost or, due to human fallibility, deliberately suppressed in certain interpretations of the Christian message. The reading of the gospel is always conditioned by circumstances of place and time. Constant serious and sincere historical rethinking or revisioning is something that should bring to light new developments, as well as needed transitions and passages that may point to fresh directions. Organizations, just as much as individuals, have to struggle with this reality of life.

To say, therefore, that Christian mission cannot be envisaged today and for the future in the same way as it was in 1911 when Maryknoll was established, or even in 1946 when Maryknollers first arrived in Africa, is for most people to state the obvious. But change in the world and in the church is what compels Christian theologians and missionary societies like Maryknoll to "rethink mission."[8] How can we envision the future of mission – and for us, specifically in the context of contemporary Africa?

The purpose of this brief presentation is to isolate and explain in summary some paradigms that are indispensable for mission today, listening to Pope John Paul II's understanding of missionary activity in *Redemptoris Missio* (no. 41) as "nothing other and nothing less than the manifestation or epiphany of God's plan and its fulfillment in the world and in history." The Pope articulates the question before the theologian: "What paths does the Church follow in order to achieve this goal?"

Trends in Mission

I will refer to these paths or paradigms of mission, necessitated by different contemporary situations, as "trends." The outlines of many of these are already discernible in the general mission vision of the church, at least in the church in Africa. Here I would like just to

---

8   For example, see Laurenti Magesa, *Rethinking Mission: Evangelization in Africa in a New Era* (Eldoret: Gaba Publications, 2006)

rearticulate them perhaps more clearly and systematically and to try to formulate the kind of action the church must adopt in each case.

A. Mission as Inculturation

When the Maryknoll Fathers arrived in Musoma in 1946, they found essentially one culture, though with various expressions. Granted that a missioner had to learn a different dialect virtually whenever he or she moved from one mission station to another, even within this small geographical area, these dialects were all African, conveying basically the same fundamental physical and spiritual cosmology. But now, just slightly over three generations later, this is no longer the case. Although today one can communicate in one language, Kiswahili, across Tanzania and more or less the whole region of East Africa, it is paradoxical that Kiswahili is itself a source of multiculturalism. The language has brought together in close proximity people of disparate origins, educational formation and cultures, not only from within the region and country, but from beyond as well. A situation like this was unthinkable only half a century ago, but is now a sign of the time.

If this is true of a district or country like Tanzania, it is much more so for the wider world: today's world is a multicultural world in every sense of the word. Rapid human mobility, the global spread of technology, and the facility of global communication, especially by electronic means, have made this possible. The trend towards oneness of the world seems irreversible.

Still, and equally paradoxically, as the world becomes one socially, the desire for social and cultural identities among different groups is becoming stronger. Different peoples seem to be consolidating their social and cultural identities, often even destructively.[9] For evangelization, this raises the question and necessity of proclaiming the gospel within local contexts, without losing sight of the global.[10] This is inculturation. Pope John Paul offers the example of St. Paul.

---

9 See Samuel P. Huntington, "The Clash of Civilizations?" in Foreign Affairs 72:3 (1993), 22-49, later expanded into *The Clash of Civilizations and the Remaking of World Order* (New York: Touchstone, 1996.

10 See Robert J. Schreiter, *The New Catholicity: Theology between the Global and the Local* (Maryknoll, New York: Orbis Books, 1997).

He writes in *Redemptoris Missio* (no. 37) that "After preaching in a number of places, St. Paul arrived in Athens, where he went to the Areopagus and proclaimed the Gospel in language appropriate to and understandable in those surroundings (cf. Acts 17:22-31). At that time the Areopagus represented the cultural center of the learned people of Athens, and today it can be taken as a symbol of the new sectors in which the Gospel must be proclaimed."

B. Mission as Dialogue

There has, of course, always existed a multiplicity of faiths and religions among the peoples of the world; but there is a renewed appreciation today in the Catholic Church concerning their status and role in the economy of salvation. Vatican II, naturally, gives priority to Judaism, but it recognizes also the importance of Islam – together with Christianity and Judaism – as constituting the Abrahamic traditions. Nevertheless, other faiths and religions are not overlooked by this Council as also agents of divine revelation. The Council urges that the great traditions of the Far East, namely, Hinduism and Buddhism, are to be given the respect they deserve in the process of God's self disclosure to the world. Although African Religion is not mentioned by name in the Council's documents, it is not difficult to infer that it is not thereby excluded. *Nostra Aetate*, the Declaration on the relationship of the church to non-Christian religions (no. 2), for example, addresses this point when it asserts that the Church "looks with sincere respect upon those [religious] ways of conduct and of life … [that] often reflect a ray of that Truth which enlightens all …"

The mission of the future cannot further ignore the relationship and collaboration between and among all those who believe in Jesus Christ, namely, the Eastern Catholic churches and the Protestant churches. As the Decree *Unitatis Redintegratio* ENGLISH (no. 3) puts it, "all those justified by faith through baptism are incorporated into Christ. They therefore have a right to be honored by the title of Christian, and are properly regarded as brothers [and sisters] in the Lord …" This is referred to as "ecumenism." In all of this, it is essential for the future of mission to keep in mind the basic requirement of the freedom of religion as an indispensable component of the dignity of the human person. No one should be coerced in any way – explicitly or otherwise – to join, abandon, or act in accordance with or against any faith or religious orientation against his or her will.[11]

Mission in this context implies dialogue, the interaction between and among people whose goal is mutual knowledge and understanding. Any other approach is oppressive and risks disrespecting human freedom and dignity and, consequently, divine will.

C. Mission as Recognition of Diversity

When the first group of Maryknoll missioners arrived in Africa in 1946, the distinction – yes, even separation – between the local and the global was still obvious. The U.S., for instance, was the U.S., and Africa was Africa. Tanganyika (present-day Tanzania) was at the time a Trust Territory of the League of Nations under Great Britain; there was no such thing as a "Tanganyika" nation. The territory was composed of hundreds of disparate ethnic groups or so-called "tribes," mostly considered by the colonialists and missionaries alike as primitive and pagan. These were people, it was thought, without any notion of culture, to be civilized and evangelized. As far as the missionaries and colonialists were concerned, they were, for all intents and purposes, "the white man's burden." I do not think there were Coca Cola drinks in the shops, that is, such "shops" as existed in a place like Musoma. I am told that compared to nowadays, the journey by ship from New York to East Africa via Cape Town took an incredibly long time!

All this is, of course, no longer the case. Again, due to technology and the means of mass communication, the world has become literally a "global village." The movement of peoples and ideas is now almost instantaneous, making claims of cultural or economic exclusivism unsustainable. Unlike in past generations, when every word out of the missioner's mouth was considered as good as an oracle, mission today must recognize diversity of opinion. The best way to teach in our age is by the example of goodness and love. In 1975, Pope Paul VI made the

---

11 See *Dignitatis Humanae (Declaration on Religious Freedom)*.

powerful comment in his Apostolic Exhortation *Evangelii Nuntiandi* (no. 41) that today people listen "more willingly to witnesses than to teachers, and if … [they do] listen to teachers, it is because they are witnesses." The kind of witness that is relevant and significant in our day involves respect, sharing and mutuality across differences. In the encyclical letter *Caritas in Veritate (Charity in Truth,* e.g. nos. 38 and 49), Pope Benedict XVI calls it simply "solidarity."

D. Primary Evangelization

The reality of the "global village" brings to the Church's attention today as never before the fact that there are still people in some areas of the world who have not had the chance to hear the gospel of Jesus Christ or to interact with Christian believers closely enough for dialogue to take place. In spite of arguments from some quarters against the ethics of primary evangelization that claim to "let each one adhere to one's religious beliefs undisturbed," Jesus' mandate to Christians to preach the gospel "to all nations" stands. Indeed, it appears that objections are often leveled against methods employed in primary evangelization rather than against the mandate itself. On the eve of the present century, Pope John Paul II recognized this and bluntly asked forgiveness for some such methods used in the past, including religious intolerance, cultural arrogance, and coercion. For him, "the Church, on its own initiative, should look again at the dark aspects of its own history, judging it in the light of the principles of the Gospel."[12] In his letter, *Tertio Millennio Adveniente* (*On the Threshold of the Third Millennium,* no. 35), he admitted that there were, indeed, extenuating circumstances for such attitudes and behavior of past centuries. Nevertheless, he insisted that admitting that they were mistakes should be a lesson to the church for the future. Citing Vatican II, he emphasized that "The truth cannot impose itself except by virtue of its own truth, as it wins over the mind [and heart] with both gentleness and power."

---

12 From a memorandum to the Cardinals in 1994. See Luigi Accattoli, *When a Pope Asks Forgiveness: The Mea Culpa's of John Paul II* (New York: Alba House, 1998), 174.

If anything, globalization impresses upon the world the necessity of sharing. To be shared are not only material but also spiritual goods, among which is the Christian gospel. The church's *missio ad extra* is closely connected with *missio ad intra:* as the Church evangelizes beyond her boundaries, she observes and absorbs into herself the presence of the divine Spirit working there. She thus becomes closer to Christ who reflects himself in the values and riches to be found in other cultures and religions.

E. New Ecclesiological Opportunity in Small Christian Communities

Speaking specifically about mission in Africa, the rise of Small Christian Communities (SCCs) – similar, though not quite identical with the Basic Ecclesial Communities (CEB) of Latin America – presents an opportunity for rethinking the ecclesiological dimension of the Christian faith that has influenced the thinking of the church since medieval times. The model of church incorporated in contemporary SCCs goes back to the early experience of the believers as described in the Acts of the Apostles (2:42): "They devoted themselves to the teaching of the apostles and to the communal life, to the breaking of the bread and to the prayers."

Incidentally, the idea of SCCs in East Africa may have been broached and developed by members of Maryknoll society in Musoma, and one of, if not *the*, foremost interpreters in Africa of the theology and pastoral implications of SCCs, happens to be a member of Maryknoll. Father Joseph G. Healey has published extensively on the subject since the official promulgation of this model of church by the region's bishops in 1976 who put it forward as the "key pastoral priority" for the church in the region. According to Healey, SCCs in Africa are not like "flying saucers" that everybody talks about but have never seen. In Africa, he notes, "We have experienced SCCs as a new model of church ..."[13]

---

13 Joseph Healey, "Innovations and New Trends in Small Christian Communities (SCCs) in Africa Today" in *Hekima Review, 40* (May 2009), 85.

F. Rethinking the Ministerial Structures of the Church in Mission

The rise of SCCs as a new way of being church has brought most powerfully to the fore the truth of the principle that in the church's *needs should determine ministries and not ministries its needs.* John Baur explains that this model of church "as People of God" – or in the image of the First African Synod, as "Family of God" – was what guided the early Church. It requires that "all the faithful fulfill their vocation and mission in the Church … implying a change from the priest-based apostolate to a people-based apostolate which demands that the priest assumes the role of a 'community minded inspirational minister.'"[14]

The shortage of priests has definitely been a concern in the church for some time now, and all indications are that the numbers of priests will continue to drop in many parts of the world. Yet, that is not the primary reason why new forms and styles of ministry should be encouraged and developed. Rather, the fundamental reason is that this development is as much an intrinsic part of the nature of the church as it is an appropriate response to the signs of the time.

G. The Role of Women in the Church, Ministry, and Mission

A reconsideration of the ministerial structure of the church is now almost universally acknowledged. It has been necessitated in recent years not least by the Feminist Movement. Described by different names in different regions, the movement is a reality all over the world. As Lisa Isherwood and Dorothea McEwan point out, despite many ideological obstacles in church and society, "Women's religious authority in Christianity, teaching the faith to their children and exceptionally so to adults, caring for the young and the old and the weak in their communities in the name of Jesus, praying and following practical and intellectual pursuits, has never been totally eradicated" from the church's consciousness.[15] It is important, however, that today this consciousness becomes doctrinally and structurally formalized.

---

14 Baur, *2000 Years*, p. 319-20

15 Lisa Isherwood and Dorothea McEwan, *Introducing Feminist Theology* (Sheffield: Sheffield Academic Press, 1993).

This is what numerous women's voices and longings indicate. Mission and ministry are not complete without the formal, visible participation of the women faithful in the Church's structures of ministry.

Everyone is aware that aspects of this question are hotly debated in and outside of the church and that many among them simply admit of no easy answers. They have risked causing dangerous rifts in the Christian community in the past. Nevertheless, discussion, even on the most controversial of them in the present shift of consciousness in mission must not be muzzled by any kind of *fiat* from above; indeed, it cannot. The only principle to keep in mind in the ongoing process is the saying popularly attributed to St. Augustine: "In essentials, unity; in doubtful matters, liberty; in all things, charity."

H. Christianity's Shift to the South and Its Implications for Mission

That in the last 75 years Christianity has shifted from the Northern to the Southern Hemisphere, at least demographically, is undisputable.[16] There are more Christians now in the South than in the North, and the trend seems to continue. But the shift is not only restricted to demography: even more significant is the fact that the South is increasingly sending missionaries to the North in reverse of what used to be the case only a few decades ago. Theologically. too, there have been in recent years major theological initiatives and developments to rival those of the North. One thinks, for example, of the ecclesial impact of Latin American Liberation Theology which flourished in the decades of the 1970s and 80s before it was restrained by the Vatican authorities in Catholic Christianity. Other initiatives pertain to the flavor of liturgical celebrations, usually marked by a festive mood characteristic of African peoples.

The implications of this shift for mission are huge. Unlike in former times when mission in terms of theology and ecclesiology was nothing more than a cultural export from the West to "the rest of us," the influence of the theological experience of the South is progressively being felt in the worldwide church, making it hard to ignore. A truly

---

16 See also Michael C. Kirwen, "Introducing the Symposium," elsewhere in this volume.

global church is, therefore, being born from the hegemonic ruins of West. This, again, necessitates dialogue and mutual theological cross-fertilization among ecclesial communities around the world.[17]

I. The Poor in Theology and Mission

The Tanzanian Catholic statesman, Julius K. Nyerere, argued in 1971 in a landmark speech to the Maryknoll Sisters that the problem of poverty in the modern world lies less in the lack of resources to provide decent life for all human beings but rather in (an often deliberate) skewed distribution of wealth within nations and internationally. As he saw things, with proper production and distribution of food, for example, there would be enough for everyone not to go hungry. The problem, however, is that structures that are in place make it almost impossible to change the situation; they ensure that some (always a minority) have too much while others (the majority) have to do with less that enough. This is an ethical question which lies at the heart of the mission of the church. Vatican II's documents, in particular *Gaudium et Spes (The Pastoral Constitution on the Church in the Modern World,* no. 1), assert as much.

In recent decades, various theologies around the world have elaborated on and developed this insight of the Scriptures. The teaching of the church on social issues in modern times has also insisted on it, taking its cue also from the early Fathers of the Church. According to the teaching of the church, the "preferential option" for the poor is a "constitutive dimension of the preaching

of the Gospel, or, in other words, [is an indispensable part] of the Church's mission for the redemption of the human race and its liberation from every oppressive situation."[18]

---

17 For example, see Richard R. Gaillardetz, *Ecclesiology for a Global Church: A People Called and Sent* (Maryknoll, New York: Orbis Books, 2008).

18 The expression comes from the 1971 synodal document "Justice in the World" (*Justitia in Mundo,* Introduction).

J. Ecological Consciousness in Mission

In *Caritas in Veritate* (no. 51), Pope Benedict XVI makes an intrinsic, cause-and-effect connection, between human behavior towards the environment and toward humanity itself. *"The way humanity treats the environment influences the way it treats itself, and vice versa,"* [19] he says. "Every violation of solidarity and civic friendship," the Pope explains, "harms the environment, just as environmental deterioration in turn upsets relations in society." By firmly linking charity, an evangelical value central to mission, and ecological consciousness and protection, Pope Benedict is warning that to ignore the issue of ecological degradation and environmental protection today is to fail in charity, in human concern. And to so fail means to shortchange God's mission, of which the Church's evangelization activity is an extension in history.

The separation between mission as evangelization and mission as ecological concern and advocacy is now redundant, according to Pope Benedict. "Nature ... is so integrated into the dynamics of society and culture that by now it hardly constitutes an independent variable," he writes (no. 51). This is why *"The Church has a responsibility towards creation*[20] and she must assert this responsibility in the public sphere," the Pope insists. "In so doing, she must defend not only earth, water and air as gifts of creation that belong to everyone. She must above all protect mankind from self-destruction" (no. 51).[21]

Conclusion

There are certainly other important considerations for mission, but these ten shifts appear to me the most deserving of our attention at this time. Ignoring any or all of them risks the danger of letting mission practice drift in unchartered waters. However, God's mission entrusted to the church deserves better attention. It needs focus, and the above paradigms provide that spotlight.

---

19 Italics in original.

20 Italics in original.

21 See also Richard J. Neuhaus, *The Naked Public Square: Religion and Democracy in America* (Grand Rapids, Michigan: Wm. B. Eerdmans Publishing Co., 1984).

The Quest for Holistic Mission

Dr. Philomena Njeri Mwaura

I feel privileged for being invited to join the Maryknoll missionaries in celebrating one hundred years of mission and sixty five of those years in Africa. I am very grateful to Fr. Lance Nadeau for requesting me to present a reflection on the future of mission in Africa in the light of the current challenges facing Africa, foremost of which are poverty, social and economic justice, human rights abuse, ethnocentrism, gender justice, exclusion, peace, reconciliation, sustainable livelihood, and total well-being, among others. This is a great milestone that comes in the wake of the centenary of the 1910 World Missionary Conference, which was commemorated in June 2010 at the Edinburg 2010 World Mission Conference, with the theme "Witnessing to Christ Today." The primary task of mission is said to be to bring people closer together regardless of race, class, caste, gender, religion and other differences. Christian mission is an act of sending and receiving someone to enable them to relate themselves to God and others through Christ. As I reflect on the proceedings of this symposium, where the context in which the Maryknoll Missionaries have been doing mission in Africa is outlined, I have been prompted to ask: What is mission today? Is it still the process of conversion? How different is mission today from the way it was conceptualized in the past? Is there a need for rethinking or re-envisioning mission? What are the markers of such mission theology? How can the Church in Africa be better equipped to carry out its missionary mandate?

This presentation will reflect on these questions, bearing in mind that mission implies the calling of the church at every level to participate in the mission of the "Triune God who created the world as an expression of love, power and creativity, who sustains and rules the universe, and who sent Jesus Christ into the world in the power of the Holy Spirit as healing, liberating savior, and who will bring about final reconciliation and restoration."[1] During this consultation, we have heard that perceptions and methods of mission and the issues of focus have changed in the last one hundred years. Motivation for engaging in mission is also under question and the genuineness of missionaries is challenged as the shift from "foreign" to "local" missionaries takes root. This presentation will begin by exploring briefly the perceptions of mission before examining the context in which mission is done in Africa, and conclude by outlining what a holistic mission would entail and which should underscore the future of mission in Africa.

Perceptions of Mission

The meaning, context and dimensions of mission have been the subject of investigation and debate by missiologists, mission practitioners and theologians, and the concept has undergone considerable paradigm shifts over the years. Perceptions of mission have changed and become multifaceted, but Jesus' imperative to proclaim the Gospel to all nations and making his disciples of them has not. Mission is not just the church's activity in another culture, local or abroad, but is a frontier of belief, conviction and commitment. The Catholic Church's understanding of mission is well articulated in the Vatican II document *Ad Gentes (Decree on the Church's Missionary Activity)*, Pope Paul VI's Apostolic Exhortation *Evangelii Nuntiandi (On Evangelization of Peoples)* and John Paul II's encyclical, *Redemptoris Missio (The Mission of the Redeemer)*, among other texts of Catholic Social Teaching. In these teachings, mission is articulated as the activity of "proclaiming Christ and his Gospel, building the

---

1 http//:www.fmc-canada.org/global/resources/theology _mission 2006 pdf. *A Theology of Mission for Free Methodist World Mission: 4.* Downloaded 26ᵗʰ May 2008.

local Church and promoting the values of the Kingdom".[2]

The teachings also reiterate that Christian mission is divine and a fundamental obligation of the church. Mission, which is also referred to as evangelization is primarily understood as an encounter of a people with the Good News of God's love proclaimed by Jesus Christ (Matt. 22:34-40; Jn. 3:16-17; 15:9-17). It entails converting, heralding or worshipping, and an involvement in the world. The context of evangelization requires a proper understanding of the notion of salvation, which implies liberation from all that oppresses and dehumanizes people, social, cultural, economic, political, spiritual or personal. Mission in this understanding means regeneration of people in a fundamental way through the power of the gospel. Evangelization should bring about inner transformation in people, thus making them new creatures who witness to God's transforming presence and activity in society. John Pobee perceives mission in an African context as enabling people to do the will of God, working for a community of communities and bringing wholeness and healing.[3]

The church is called to participate in this integral mission of God from wherever she is located and in the power of the Holy Spirit. The church is said to be by its very nature missionary; it exists by mission as a fire by burning. Mission creates the church and bridges the gap between the church and the Kingdom of God. The church is called into being by the Father "who so loved the world that he gave his only Son that whoever believes in Him shall not perish but have eternal life" (Jn. 3:16) and who sent the Holy Spirit to lead believers into truth.[4] The church is centered and grounded in the word and is a communion of those who, by their encounter with the word, stand in a living relationship with God. The church is defined by its common partaking in the life of God who is Trinity and is the source and focus of every communion. It is both a divine and human institution. Although the church is made up of human beings who are members of one body of

---

2 John Paul II, *Redemptoris Missio*, no. 33.

3 John S. Pobee, "Lord, Creator-Spirit, Renew and Sustain the Whole Creation," *International Review of Mission*, 29 (April 1990):55

4 WCC, *The Nature and Mission of the Church: A Stage in the Way to a Common Statement* (Geneva: WCC, 2005), 11.

Christ and open to the free activity of the Holy Spirit, in its human condition it is still subject to the conditions of the world.

In this regard, as the World Council of Churches observes, the church is open to change which, though it leads to positive and negative developments, is open to decline and distortion. It is also open to the power of sin and to individual, cultural and historical conditioning which can contribute to a richness of insights and expressions of faith, but also to relativising tendencies or to absolutising particular views.[5]

It is, therefore, crucial that the church becomes attuned to the signs of the times in order to creatively respond to changed situations with new understandings and attitudes about the mission mandate. Questions have been raised about missionary methods and the attitudes generated by these methods in the minds of the evangelizers and the evangelized, despite the fact that the legitimacy of mission has not been questioned, at least in Africa. What is the context in which Christians participate in God's mission in Africa? Is mission still necessary? How effective is it?

The Necessity of Mission for Africa

Africa is a context that tells two stories that are diametrically opposed. One is a story of frustration and cry of children, women and men who are tired of unending poverty, gender based violence, who desperately seek to end the misery caused by civil wars, ethnic conflicts, debilitating disease, including HIV and AIDS, and mismanagement of national affairs and resources. The other story is one of a vibrant Christianity, a rich spirituality that engenders hope and sustains her in the midst of this apparent chaos. There is joy in community life and the African values of solidarity, mutual caring, reverence for God, and a dynamic engagement with spiritual forces is experienced and shared. Nevertheless, the church is so fragmented that there is not much sustained ecumenical cooperation or interfaith dialogue. It is as if night and day existed simultaneously in modern Africa.

---

5   WCC, *The Nature and Mission,* 30.

It is an acknowledged fact that Christianity is growing tremendously in Africa. To quote some statistics which may not be very reliable yet give crucial indicators: during the twentieth century, the proportion of Africans who were Christians in the world rose from 9% of the whole to almost half. According to the *World Christian Encyclopedia*, "African Christians have mushroomed from 9.9 million (0.6%) of the world's population, to 300 million in AD 2000 (89%).The present net increase on the continent is 8.4 million new Christians a year (23,000 a day) of which 1.5 million are net new converts."[6] Just like in the rest of the Two Thirds World, what is drawing Africans to Christianity is the power of the gospel to change the individual and one's personal circumstances, and a search for the key to social transformation of the modern world. The gospel message of justice and love of God for the poor and marginalized resonates with a context that is characterized by struggles for survival and for justice and peace.

There is tremendous revival in the church as is evidenced by multiplication of new Pentecostal Christian groups and charismatic renewal movements within Protestant and Catholic christianities. Unfortunately, numerical growth has not resulted into a transforming spirituality that fosters Christian and national identity. Ethnicity is a demon threatening to tear not only the nation state apart, but also the church. The church also needs to address social-economic, cultural, socio-political concerns, ecumenism, minorities, migration, inter-religious dialogue, violence, gender injustice and environmental degradation, among others, as crucial issues, if her missionary engagement is to be fruitful. It has been recognized that the church's initiative in welfare provision, emergency relief, pastoral care and general presence among the hurting is commendable, but its prophetic witness leaves much to be desired. The leadership ought to listen more and establish structures of ministry that put the poor at the center of mission, accompany them, and be in solidarity with them in their struggle for liberation. "Poor" here means those on the margins, the excluded, be they refugees, migrants, economically poor, women, children, youth, aged, minorities, and so

---

6   David B.Barrett et al., *World Christian Encyclopedia: Comparative Survey of Churches and Religions in the Modern World.* Vol. 1, Second Edition (New York: Oxford University Press, 2001), 5.

on. Current ecclesiology also needs thorough evaluation for the model of church determines how Christians understand themselves and their roles in it. There are other challenges facing the church in Africa. Allow me to briefly outline them.

More Challenges

The issue of ethnic conflicts and violence pervades much of Africa. Today, nineteen of the fifty-four African nations are either experiencing conflicts, wars, or are undergoing post-conflict reconstruction. While we may thank God that the church is growing numerically, vocations to the priesthood and religious life are increasing; the depth of faithful commitment, as already mentioned, is something to diligently work on. This makes the task of reconciliation, justice and peace a matter of utmost concern and priority. There should be mission focus on ways to promote genuine peace, built on justice and development. The church's involvement in peace building, conflict resolution, peace and civic education, anti-gun campaigns, and advocacy for human rights and economic justice is remarkable. However more spirited effort is required centered not on secular approaches but gospel ones.

Another issue related to the promotion of human dignity is that of the HIV and AIDS pandemic and gender justice. The HIV and AIDS pandemic requires a more holistic approach, not just as a medical and moral issue, but one of social justice, considering that it is aggravated by poverty which is a result of bad governance and other macro factors. The church generally has not addressed gender questions, which are not just about ordination of women. The critical concern is about involving women in decision making at all levels, promoting the rights of the girl child (as well as the boy child), addressing gender based violence as a moral, theological and social issue, and teaching of the equal dignity of women in sermons, catechetical training, and Small Christian Communities discussions. To continually be relevant, the church needs to continue her advocacy for social justice, equitable distribution of resources, and the promotion of the dignity of the person in teaching and practice. Economic growth in some countries like Kenya, Malawi, Zambia, South Africa, Tanzania and Uganda in the last five years has not translated into marked improvement in the livelihoods of people. It has widened the gap between the rich and poor classes, and the frustration of the people has been expressed through ethnic and xenophobic violence as witnessed in Kenya and South Africa, especially in 2008.

Mission should, therefore create a balance between service provision, proclamation of the gospel and being prophetic. Former mission churches also require to be more self reliant in theology, mission practice and other areas. This calls for a creative and dynamic view of mission and accountability even in church affairs. Peter Henriot, writing about the Catholic Church in Zambia, observes: "... we still have a long way to go before we can say that mechanisms of participation, guarantee of human rights and openness of decision making are fully adopted in the Church."[7]

Towards a Holistic Mission

Although the future of mission is ultimately in God's hands, it is the privilege of human beings to shape it based on the understanding of the past and present. The church, as this symposium has made clear, is constitutive of the whole people of God, individuals and groups responding to the law of Christ, whose eternal element is the invitation to express love to others. The church continues to renew itself and its mission too. For any individual or group to live fully involves correcting mistakes of the past and charting a better vision of the future. This is even more imperative for Christians in the spirit of repentance or *metanoia*. What does this mean in practical terms? In the face of seemingly hopeless and precarious situations of conflict, war, disease, and social injustice, how can the church live and engage in its mission in such a manner as to be a sign and instrument of change and hope that is rooted in the Paschal mystery? The rest of this reflection will focus on five areas which to me are of major concern for this symposium.

---

7   Peter Henriot, "AMECEA and the Second African Synod," *New People,* 114 (May – June 2008): 20.

Promoting Peace-building, Justice and Reconciliation

The deep hurts and painful experiences that the African continent has experienced invite the church to mediate peace, reconciliation and healing. It calls for an ecumenical mission and vision that entails partnering in pain by accompanying our members who are suffering, whether it is ill health through HIV and AIDS, ethnic conflicts, gender violence, child abuse, or any other form of suffering. We should not as people of God fail in our moral duty to stand up for justice and speak out where it is violated. Ethnic hatred and xenophobia are a great hindrance to the church's mission to live the life of love of Christ in Africa. Its major source is the problem of "otherness," which regards those unlike "us" as less human or unworthy. This "othering" extends to differences such as gender, class, race and even religion/faith. Difference should not be divisive but should be celebrated. The church should reflect on this concept of otherness and foster what Miroslav Volf calls a "theology of embrace." He observes that "The future of the whole world depends on how we deal with ethnic, religious and gender otherness."[8] Volf points out the inability to relate the core theological beliefs about reconciliation to the shape of the church's social responsibility.

Furthermore, individualized, pietistic and evangelical Christianity (prevalent in Europe) has placed little focus on social reconciliation: faith is a matter of the soul's relationship with God and lacks a social dimension. An exclusive emphasis on private morality based on an individual's reconciliation with God leads to an aversion towards the world and the other. Could this be the problem   at the root of ethnic animosity among Christians? The social dimension of reconciliation was central to human and communal relationships in Africa. This is a resource the church can tap into as it evolves new dynamic ways of being church and as it addresses injustice, social and political strife.

The church in Africa should see her mission as bringing wholeness to people as Jesus did. Jesus' ministry was grounded in *Shalom,* an Old Testament concept of peace that is inclusive of harmony and wellbeing.

---

8   Miroslav Volf, cited in Anne-Marie Kool, "The Church in Hungary, Central and Eastern: Trends and Challenges," *The Princeton Seminary Bulletin,* XXVIII: 2 (2007): 149.

Shalom entails justice, healed relations between individuals in the society, between God and humanity, and between humanity and the rest of creation. The greatest challenge is post war/conflict reconstruction. This is where confession, forgiveness, reconciliation and healing are necessary. This reconciliation should not be a hasty process but one that respects and restores human dignity. It should be seen as a process that leads victims to discover the mercy of God welling up their lives. It is discovering God's reconciliation through Christ. It is allowing the Holy Spirit to bring forgiveness and reconciliation among people who are hurting, both victims and perpetrators. As Esther Mombo asserts, "for reconciliation to be there, the victim must forgive, the perpetrators cannot forgive themselves. That forgiveness must carry something of the unboundedness of grace that God gives. We must not count trespasses more than God does."[9]

Discipling the Nations

Commenting on the apparent superficiality and nominality of African Christianity, Madu says that as long as Africa's cherished ideals and values are not met by the gospel, then its cogency for the African becomes questionable and Africans will continue to ask, "Is this the Christ or shall we look for another?"[10] This is a challenge to an uninculturated evangelization. The future of mission and the church in Africa depends on the sound, committed and honest theological reflection and not mere numerical strength. There is need for comprehensive, integrated and systematic ongoing formation catechesis, the emphasis of which should not be only on intellectual learning of the faith but also on living it; a catechesis that facilitates a living personal and communal encounter with the risen Lord. This will promote moral behavior and mutual concern and responsibility.

The Good News is about transforming cultures as well. When people have the Good News and turn to God in Jesus Christ, they express their

---

9 Esther Mombo, "Building a Culture of Peace Through Reconciliation from a Christian Religious Perspective," in *Overcoming Violence: A Faith Based Response*, ed. Mary N. Getui and W. Musyoni (Nairobi: NCCK. 2004),144.

10 Madu Emeka, "The Place of African Culture on Christian Practice: Food for Thought for Nigeria's Major Seminaries," *African Christian Studies*, 19: 3 (2003): 34.

response creatively in a new way to community, structures, rituals and celebrations, reflection and spirituality. Doing mission in a holistic and transformational manner implies surrendering ourselves to Christ to be purified, sanctified and renewed. It entails Christ confronting and transforming our lives and institutions to be like him. Until the gospel effects this transformation through being inculturated in the African context; we shall continue lamenting about an "uncompleted mission," "superficial gospel," and a "schizophrenic Christianity." A sustained theological engagement and formation is the major challenge to Christian mission in Africa.

Prophetic Leadership

For effective mission, there is need for a courageous, empowered and committed leadership. Our church leaders should have pastoral integrity. A leader should have a stand, be dependable, uphold justice, and have convictions and courage. Church leaders should embody in their leadership, just like Jesus, integrity, dignity and humility. The Kenyan church has been accused of failing to provide prophetic leadership during the 2005 referendum on the draft constitution, December 2007 General Elections that resulted in violence, and allegedly taking sides in the political crises that engulfed the nation in late 2007 and early 2008. Theological education/formation is crucial to developing this type of leadership. A visionary leadership is required that is able to engage in a dynamic and informed way with the myriad of issues confronting the African continent.

Dialogue as a Way of Mission

Africa is a continent of diverse nations, cultures and religions. Expressing integrity in mission entails an awareness of this pluralistic context and recognizing that Christians can only fulfill their mission mandate in collaboration. Dialogue has not been a common practice in the church due to fundamentalist currents and misuse of the power of religion by economic and political vested interests. We, however, need to listen to one another in order to effectively proclaim the Good News. In the process of mutual listening, there is mutual learning and our common experience of God is deepened. This also facilitates common living, while respecting the dignity and differences of others.

Witness to the Marginalized

For the church's mission in Africa to be relevant, it must be inclusive and bring *Shalom,* God's peace, to the marginalized. To be church in Africa is to have "good news" for the crowd of humanity that seeks fullness of life without ever achieving it, the poor, and the deprived rural and urban poor, and especially pastoralists. These are the victims of economic and political injustices, women, men and children. Women and the girl child are especially oppressed by patriarchy both in church and society. Reconstructing mission calls for dismantling of patriarchal notions and power structures that prevents people from experiencing the liberative power of God. This would also lead to attentiveness of what women bring and can bring to the church. In an insightful article on the church and AIDS, A. E. Orobator observes that "in the context of AIDS, the face of the Church as a mult-sectoral, ministering and healing community has a distinctively feminine profile. This profile or face embodies an important aspect of the Church's identity and mission namely Church as mother."[11]

This dimension is visible in the many ways that women provide care to the infected and affected. The spiritual and social accompaniment, compassion and commitment provided by these women in responding to AIDS are integral to the identity and mission of the church. The same can be said of women as healers and peace makers in conflict situations. A renewed or reconstructed mission should value the contribution of women in all situations and accord them greater freedom in representing the profound reality of church as mother to the rest of society. A renewed church should deconstruct the structures of gender based discrimination in church and society. The image of the church as a caring community is tarnished by its abetting, knowingly or inadvertently, the oppression and discrimination of women.

The youth is another forgotten category by the church and society. They are acclaimed as leaders of tomorrow but they wait forever to

---

11 Agbonkhianmeghe E. Orobator, "When AIDS Comes to the Church" in *AIDS in Africa: Theological Reflections*, ed. Benezet Bujo and M. Czerny (Nairobi: Paulines Publications Africa, 2007), 124.

take the mantle from their parents. They are a resource that the church is not adequately utilizing. The modern missionary movement owes its success to the committed and untiring efforts of youth world wide through organizations like the Young Men Christian Association, Young Women Christian Association, World Student Christian Federation, Student Christian Movement, and so on. I understand that the youth department is the most under funded and undervalued department in many churches. This needs to change. It is not surprising that young people are moving to charismatic churches which have relatively younger membership and provide more fulfilling opportunities for participation and leadership. Unfortunately, there are also youth who drop out of one church and do not join any other. Some have also never been evangelized. These are the ones who become fodder for politicians in urban and rural areas. This is a frontier of mission, especially in urban slums, that needs serious attention. It has been observed that many mainline churches are reluctant to engage in "slum ministry" and the church in the slums does not perceive itself as part of the local church. Most of the clergy serving in urban slums are foreign missionaries. The local church is therefore challenged to be inclusive.

Conclusion

The church in Africa is growing, as evidenced by the number on Christians in the continent, the increase in vocations, the number of local clergy, educational, health and pastoral institutions, and development of projects and programmes aimed at uplifting the lives of the people. Mission in terms of proclamation and witness has, therefore, succeeded. However, it is lamented that this numerical growth is not matched by moral transformation of people as is visible in the frequent and persisting ethnic conflicts, corruption, impunity, and disregarded for healthy relationships among fellow human beings. Mission is not a state, it is a process, an ongoing task. We too are not Christians but continually become Christians. Therefore, discipling is an ongoing task if Christians have to love and live the life Christ calls us to. To the question, "Africa, where are you headed?" I respond that there is need for a renewed vision for mission. It is one that must change Africa's destiny so that reconciliation will overcome hatred and divisions, and peace and justice will finally reign. It is a vision that calls for imagining another possible world centered on Christ who is the fullness of life, our Reconciler, our Peace, our Justice, and our Hope.

Dr. Philomena Njeri Mwaura is a Senior Lecturer in the Department of Philosophy and Religious Studies at Kenyatta University in Nairobi, Kenya. She is a former President of the International Association for Mission Studies and currently the Co-coordinator of the Theology Commission of the Ecumenical Association of Third World Theologians, Africa Region, and a member of the Circle of Concerned African Women Theologians and the East African Ecumenical Theological Symposium. She has also been an adjunct Lecturer at Akrofi Christaller Institute of Mission Research and Applied Theology, Ghana; Daystar University; Hekima College Jesuit School of Theology; and the Catholic University of Eastern Africa, in Kenya. She is a prolific researcher and writer and has published both locally and internationally. She has also co-authored text books on Christian Religious Education for the primary, secondary and teacher education curriculum in Kenya.

The Credibility of the Church Doing Mission in Africa

Rev. Peter Mamuli Nyongesa

When we ask about the credibility of the church, we have in mind the trustworthiness, the indubitable integrity of the church as messenger of the Kingdom of God.[1]

This credibility is of the utmost importance. It is true that the coming of the Kingdom is not brought about by the church itself. The salvation of humanity and the redemption of the world is the gracious work of God through his word and spirit. It is only the Holy Spirit who can kindle faith in the hearts of men. Faith is called fourth by the living Word of the living God, but even so the church is the instrument of his redemptive activity. It proclaims the Word and bears witness to the truth of the gospel. And this is when its credibility becomes important.

One could argue that the gospel is something objective, a truth that can be proclaimed and believed quite apart from those who proclaim it. In that case the credibility of the messenger would have no real importance for those called to faith. But that would be fallacious. I would not presume to say that it is impossible for God to do this. He could use the testimony of a man without any real faith in the gospel to save somebody else. But that is not the way God usually works. As a rule the Spirit uses not only

---

1 Costas Orlando, *The Church and Its Mission: A Shattering Critique from the Third World* (Wheaton, Illinois: Tyndale, 1974), 8-10, 21-57.

the words of the gospel, but also the personal evidence of the quality of the messenger to persuade men to believe.[2]

The gospel comes to us through the normal process of communication. In this process the credibility of the communicator is of the utmost importance. In preaching the gospel we do not communicate objective truths in an abstract way, but testify to the saving power of the gospel in our own lives. Something of the communicator is conveyed along with the message. The message functions within the situation in which it is proclaimed, one where the credibility of the messenger cannot be ignored. Although one cannot contend that the truth of the gospel depends on the trustworthiness of the preacher, this may be a factor in the contact between the listener and the word. In the same way the preacher's lack of credibility may obstruct the gospel by creating an unnecessary stumbling block to the acceptance of the word of God.

This is the reason why the New Testament warns explicitly against the danger of placing an obstacle in the way of one's faith in the gospel (cf. 2 Cor. 6:3). Paul urges the Corinthians not to be a cause of stumbling either to Jews or to Gentiles (1 Cor. 10:32). He takes great pains to clear himself of false accusations because he is convinced that there should be no doubt about his good faith among the churches. Especially in his second letter to the Corinthians, he defends his credibility at length. He knows too well that he has a duty to live up to his high calling and not allow anything to cast a shadow of doubt on his sincerity and integrity.

Paul knows what harm the Pharisees did to the cause of God by their lack of credibility. He knows all too well the danger of paying lip service to the law of God while at the same time trampling its commandments underfoot. In his letter to the Romans CH ?? 17-24), he hits out at the Jews: "You call yourself a Jew; you depend on the law and boast about God; you know what God wants you to do, and you have learned from the law to choose what is right; you are sure that you are a guide for the blind, a light for those who are in the darkness, an instructor for the foolish, and a teacher for the ignorant

---

2   Howard A. Snyder, *The Community of the King* (Downers Grove, Illinois: Intervarsity Press, 1977), 103-105.

...; you teach others – why don't you teach yourselves? ... You boast about having Gods law – but do you bring shame on God by breaking his law? Scripture says, "because of you Jews, the Gentiles speak evil of God'." The tragic aspect of all this is that lack of credibility in those who regard themselves as teachers of the law has results directly opposite to their intentions. They think that they are persuading outsiders to see the glory of their God and the magnificence of his law, but they have a terrible effect: the name of God is derided by the Gentiles because of what they observe in the lives of the Jews.

In the same way Christ himself reproached the Pharisees, saying that they kept the key to the door of the house of knowledge but they themselves would not go in, and so they prevented others from entering (Lk. 11:52). Clearly, it is not enough to teach the law in an objective sense. One cannot tell others the way but refuse to follow it oneself; what you say about the way may be perfectly true, but it will have no persuasive power if you lack credibility. That is why Christ chastised the teachers of the law for putting heavy loads on peoples' backs while they would not lift a finger in carrying the loads themselves (Lk. 11:46). They did not practice what they preached (Mt. 23:3). They taught others but they did not teach themselves. No wonder that their preaching had so little impact, and what effect it had was questionable: "How terrible for you teachers of the law and Pharisees! You hypocrites! You sail the seas and across whole countries to win one convert; and when you succeed, you make him twice as deserving of going to hell as you yourself are!" (Mt. 23:15).

It would be very naïve to imagine that these warnings of scripture have no message for the church in Kenya or East Africa. If we look back on the history of the church, no one can deny that a tremendous accomplishment was achieved in evangelizing the world. But we may never know the reverse side: how many people have been kept away from Christ by the church, exactly because it did not manage to present a credible witness to the saving power of the gospel. The church may do well to heed the bitter attack on Christianity by a man like Soren Kierkegaard, who pointed out clearly how far the official religion of the churches had departed from the original faith, thereby destroying their credibility. But it is not even necessary to read his Journals written in the 19th century to convince ourselves of the urgent need for a more credible church. We need only take note of sentiments of the independent churches in the East Africa, and especially in our own country, Kenya. To many members of the established churches it is a severe shock to learn what a poor image they have among the younger churches. They feel offended and betrayed when they are accused of lacking credibility. They tend to see these critical remarks as ingratitude for what they had done for the African Independent churches. But they should ask themselves how this impression of poor credibility has arisen. And they should do some soul-searching to ascertain whether they do not, perhaps unwittingly, create this impression themselves.

The matter is serious, especially at this critical stage of our history in Kenya. Africa is in the throes of a fierce struggle for a new identity. New ideologies and religions are competing for the heart of the Africa of the future. There is no doubt that the Christian faith is a major factor in this struggle and that Christianity is spreading rapidly in Africa. But it is a matter of grave concern that at this crucial time the churches in Kenya, some of whom have spent much energy and effort on spreading the gospel, should obstruct the message of Christ because of their lack of credibility. We may miss the boat; we may find ourselves disqualified from the contest, as the apostle Paul feared could happen even to him should he fail to live up to the demands of his calling (1Cor. 9:27).

What the Church should do

The question is what the church should do to gain credibility in doing mission. Surely it cannot depend on its credibility to everybody and specifically to the unbelieving world. If so, it would have to sacrifice its identity, become untrue to the gospel and conform to the convictions and the ways of the natural man. Some people fear that this is implied in the demand for credibility. But that is manifestly not so. On the contrary, the church is bound to lose credibility if it confuses this with acceptability to the world, for as soon as the church becomes not more than a rubber stamp endorsing the opinions of the world, it has nothing to offer, and it will not be taken seriously. Not even the world to which it is conforming will have any respect for it.[3] The credibility of the church in doing mission in East Africa is irrevocably linked with its faithfulness to its nature as the nature of Christ and herald of his Kingdom. Consequentially, its credibility cannot be divorced from its very willingness to be a stumbling block to many, to be out of step with general trends in the world, to give the offense and go against the grain of natural man. In one sense the church in Kenya will always be and should be unacceptable to the world. In as much as it is true to its nature as the body of Christ it shares Christ's relationship with the world. If Christ was not acceptable to the world, if he offended it and provoked its anger and hatred, the true church will do the same in East Africa. The gospel is not a human creation and will always be a stumbling block to the flesh (Gal.1:11). Those who are dominated by the flesh cannot grasp the things of the spirit (Rom.8:5-7). Without the spirit of God man cannot understand the message of the gospel and must be repelled by it because its value can be judged only in spiritual terms (1 Cor. 2:14).

Hence, it is paradoxically true that the credibility of the church in doing mission in East Africa goes hand in hand with its unacceptability to the world; at the same time, it is true that even the unconverted world is acutely sensitive to any lack of credibility in the church. Perhaps it is because the world is naturally disinclined towards the message of the church that it cannot detect its lack of credibility unerringly.[4] As long as the church retains its credibility, however, even the world will know that it is confronted with something worthwhile, although it may reject the actual message. But when the world gets the impression that the church is not trustworthy, it triumphantly scorns the church and its message.

It is true that this credibility is not discernible to the unbeliever in the same way as it is to the believer who is convinced by the Holy Spirit

---

3   Henry Bettenson, *Documents of the Christian Church* (New York: Oxford University Press, 1947), 298.

4   David O. Moberg, *The Church as a Social Institution* (Englewood Cliffs, New Jersey: Prentice-Hall, 1962), 6.

of the truth of the gospel and is therefore able to measure credibility by these standards. There is no neutral, obvious criterion for the credibility of the church that can be used by believers and unbelievers alike, just as there are no neutral, rational criteria to determine the truth of the gospel. The Holy Spirit persuades us of the latter and of the credibility of the church when the church is obviously true to the gospel it proclaims.[5] But even then the unbelieving world cannot remain untouched by the true credibility of the church. Wherever it exists, the world will have to take heed of it even if only for the church's obstinacy in adhering to its convictions and its irritating way of taking its message seriously. Although few things repel the world more than this very persistence, it instills a secret respect even among those to whom the church is a stench of death (2 Cor. 2:15-16). This may further a change of heart wherever it pleases the Holy Spirit to effect it.

The reverse is equally true in East Africa. The church should not try to win sympathy of the world by bending over backwards to obtain credibility, doing and saying things to placate the world. Sometimes the words of Paul are quoted in this regard. He says that he has made himself everybody's slave to win as many people as possible. That is why he became a Jew to the Jews, and so on (1 Cor. 9). However, it would be wrong to infer that Paul tempered with the gospel to make it acceptable to as many people as possible. He merely states that he put himself in the place of those to whom he had to preach in order to communicate the gospel to them in the clearest possible way. The gospel cannot be credible to people if it is not brought to them pertinently in a way that it is relevant to their need. But it is something quite different to adapt the gospel to human tastes.[6]

The Image of the Church

In a general sense we can say that the church in east Africa is credible when she corresponds to, or at least strives to correspond to the image

---

5 Costas Orlando, *The Church and Its Mission: A Shattering Critique from the Third World* (Wheaton, Illinois: Tyndale, 1974), 120-134.

6 Howard A. Snyder, *The Community of the King* (Downers Grove, Illinois: Intervarsity Press, 1977), 120-143.

of Christ proclaimed. It is necessary, however, to stress a few specific aspects of this image in order to get a clearer picture of what the New Testament itself teaches in this respect. I would like to single out three aspects because of their relevance to our situation. These are: the *alien character* of the church in the world, its *veracity* and its *love*.

First of all, the alien character of the church in the New Testament is very clear from the point that the church is in the world, but not of it (Jn. 17:14-18). Christians are citizens of heaven and do not belong to this world (Phil. 3:20). There is no permanent city for them on earth; they are looking for a city which is to come (Heb. 13:14). Especially, the first letter of Peter (1 Pet. 2:11) stresses the fact that Christians are strangers and fugitives in the world. They are not ordinary citizens. They have no vested rights. Therefore, they should not be surprised at the persecutions they are suffering as though it were something strange, for they are merely sharing the sufferings of Christ (1 Pet. 4:12-13). If the world hated Christ and crucified him, it is only logical that it will hate and persecute true Christians, for the servant is not greater than the master (Jn. 15:20). Theologically, the church is eschatological, being a new creation, the first fruit of the new age to come (cf. 2 Cor. 5:17, Eph. 2:10, 5:24). It follows that it will always be treated as an alien body by the world as long as it remains true to its nature. If this does not happen, then either the whole world has been converted – which is impossible – or the church has compromised with the world.

One of the manifestations of credibility to the world is the inability to judge according to the standards of God's word. Credibility, trustworthiness and loyalty do not mean what these concepts would mean if the church's primary concern was for the kingdom of God. The standard here is no longer the credibility of Jesus and the apostles. Instead, a man is called credible and trustworthy if he is loyal to the national interests and can be relied upon not to betray the national cause. He must say and do nothing that might embarrass the leaders of the church and state, or that may play into the hands of the enemies of the state. He should not criticize either the church or state too harshly since this may be detrimental to the common cause.

Once a church starts moving in this direction, it is no longer able to preserve the proper distance between itself and the world. It foregoes its foreign character. It cannot remain objective towards the truth, nor impartial in the sense of judging the problems that confront it in the light of God's word. Its credibility is at stake. The church must never identify with any earthly cause to the extent of losing its power of being faithful to the divine word in all circumstances.

The temptation of a respectable place in society, of honor and security, must not be underestimated, but the price seems to be that the church will have to compromise at least some of its convictions. I do not know of any historical examples of churches that were able to withstand this temptation in ordinary circumstances. Let us not be so naive as to expect any better from those who pour scorn on the church for its weakness in this respect and demand a new political theology. If I understand the proponents of such a theology correctly, they occupy much the same position. They merely settle for the other alternative by siding with the revolutionary powers instead of the establishment and by identifying with new national or class interests. Of course, they substantiate their case with biblical arguments and much of what they say may be true, but the same can be said of the champions of the old political religion. The crux of the matter is that either way the eschatological nature of the church is betrayed. The church can easily become the pawn of the left as of the right, and in either event loses its credibility. I do not agree with an assertion often made in our times that a true church would be partisan in that it should choose the side of the oppressed, the underprivileged or the por. It is said to have been the choice of Christ, but this may be a subtle shift in the emphasis laid in Jesus' compassion on the side of the underprivileged in the New Testament. He did not regard them as a distinct class with which he sided in opposition to the oppressors and the rich. His compassion embraced the rich as well. He came to save all men and to free them from evil, not to become involved in the class struggle. If the church chooses to do so, it will remain in the same basic position occupied by the state and national churches of the latest dispensation. This might give it a sense of credibility with the particular group it supports, but in the long run it will pay the price.

Love of the Church

The last aspect that I want to mention is the love of the church. Perhaps more than anything else, the credibility of the church in doing missions hinges on the quality of its love. There is a remarkable word of Christ in the Gospel of John (13:34-35): "And now I give you a new commandment: love for one another. As I have loved you, so you must love one another. If you have love for one another, then everyone will know that you are my disciples."

It is strange that Christ speaks about the new commandment in this connection. The commandment to love one's neighbor was well known in the Old Testament and Christ himself summarized the whole law in the twofold commandment of love (Mt. 22).[7] But what is at stake here is not just general neighborly love, but specifically brotherly love. When a Jew read in Leviticus (19:18) that he should love his neighbor as himself, he might have thought only of his fellow Jews. That mistake was corrected by Christ in the Sermon on the Mount when he stated that one should love also one's enemies (Mt. 5:43-48). This is further illustrated in the parable of the Good Samaritan, (Lk. 10:25-37). Anyone who crosses one's path is included in this commandment. The church should therefore regard all men with love and compassion and should demonstrate this in word and deed. But when we read in John (13:34) about the new commandment of love, this is obviously not just a repetition of the general command to love one's neighbor. It is a new command because it is given with a view to the new situation of the church. The church is a new creation, a totally different and unique community unlike any other community on the earth. It is the body of Christ, the foretaste of the promised renewal of all things. In this new community the love of God should be reflected. The church is the new creation of the spirit of God. And the spirit is the bond of love between the Eternal Father and the External Son, shed abroad in our hearts to unite all members of the body of Christ in the love of God. By the spirit of God they are united to God in love, but they are also united to each other by that same divine love.

---

7   Rick Love, *Muslims Magic and the Kingdom of God* (Pasadena, California: William Carey Library, 2000), 169.

Perhaps there is nothing more fundamental that can be said about the church. The true mark of the church of Christ is his love manifested in the brotherly love between its members. We are used to saying that the marks of the true church are its faithful preaching of the gospel, proper administration of the sacraments and maintenance of church discipline. In itself that is quite correct. But we should not forget that all these are meaningless without love (1 Cor. 13). It is remarkable that Article 29 of the Confessio Belgica, after enumerating these familiar external signs of the church, continues to talk about the characteristics of the true members of the church, such as faith and love, willingness to crucify the flesh, and so on. The message of the church will continue to lack credibility if it is not manifestly filled with the love of God. If the church is saved by the message of love, it should reflect that same love in its daily life as a brotherhood and sisterhood.[8] Christ said: "Everyone will know that you are my disciples if you love one another." The missionary witness of the church depends not only on what the church says, but also on what it is. The mutual love of the members of the body of Christ is a powerful testimony to the saving power of the gospel.

Hence, it is not surprising that the New Testament constantly stresses the unity of the church.[9] This is a unity of love because it derives from the Spirit. It should transcend all the barriers that normally divide people. In Christ there is no difference between Jews and Gentiles, between slaves and free men and women, because all are one in Christ Jesus (Gal. 3:28). In his second letter to the Corinthians Paul points out that if a man is in Christ he is a new being. Within the church of Christ, where we are concerned not with the old man but with the new, we do not judge according to human standards (2 Cor. 5:16-17). The reconciliation brought about by Christ does not mean only that we are changed from being God's enemies to become his friends; it also implies that men of all kinds are welded together in friendship. Christ included men of the most divergent background in his small

---

8   Love, *Muslims Magic and the Kingdom of God*, 169-171.

9   Howard A. Snyder, *The Community of the King* (Downers Grove, Illinois: Intervarsity Press, 1977), 66.

body of apostles. Zealots and tax collectors could be brought together in a new bond of love. Something of the New Age of peace prevailed wherever Jesus was. And the same holds true of the church. The Spirit of God frees men from hatred and prejudice and fills them with love and peace. In a divided, strife-torn world in which everybody seeks his own benefit and where hatred and envy are tearing men apart, the church should present a sign of the great renewal that is to come.

Perhaps nothing can do more harm to the church's credibility in the world than its lack of love and unity. The church should be a messenger or reconciliation in word and deed, but in reality it is divided against itself, unwilling to accept fellow-Christians as brothers in Christ and to practice the communion of saints. If the church were filled with the Spirit of God, it would be able to deal with existing differences in a new way. Mere external bonds of unity are meaningless; they have nothing in common with the true unity of the spirit.

Such unity will never convince the world of the reality of the message of the church that God can really change men and make them willing to accept one another in unselfish love. But that is not the unity we are talking about. We are talking about a unity of love that is a fruit of the Holy Spirit. The credibility of the church is at stake if it does not strive for such unity.

One of the worst frustrations of our time in Kenya and East Africa is the way some people oppose the idea of a meaningful manifestation of church unity by arguing that what is required is only a unity of love, and therefore invisible. But they are evading the real issue, which is that spiritual unity, the unity of love, should manifest itself in visible relationships, in the communion of saints, in mutual acceptance as brothers and sisters in Christ in such a way that the world may see that the prejudices of natural man no longer dictate our way of life. To say that such visible unity is prompted only by political rather than spiritual motives is to miss the point completely. It is the Holy Spirit who urges us to find a deeper level of unity than the bonds of kinship and culture in order to experience that the true unity of the church is much more than a human fabrication. It is the unity of love that manifests itself spontaneously and visibly in new relationships, mutual understanding and mutual service, creating the organizational structures that are necessary to protect it.

Conclusion

Meaningful unity can only come about through the Spirit of God. But as long as we do not seek such a spiritual unity of love, the church will lack credibility. Perhaps we will never achieve the full unity of the church in this world, which is after all a fallen one. But we should at least strive to be filled more and more by' the fruits of the Spirit. We should not be content with our attainments. What is more, in Kenya we should not try to invent theories explaining why we should not have more of the power of the Holy Spirit who alone can move men to accept the message of reconciliation in all its implications. The worst we could do would be to show no discomfiture at the present situation. A church that does not bemoan its lack of credibility is a fair example of what this lack means. But if we would allow the Spirit of God to take full possession of us we may – please God – be made anew.

Rev. Dr. Peter Mamuli Nyongesa is a priest of the Anglican Diocese of Bungoma and is currently the Protestant Students' Chaplain at Kenyatta University. He received his Ph.D in Theology from Potchefstroom University, South Africa, with a specialization in Missiology. He studied under the reknowned missiologist David Bosch.

PART IV
CONCLUDING REMARKS

His Grace Archbishop Allan Lebeaupin
The Apostolic Nuncio To Kenya

I would like to thank the Maryknoll Society of Priests and Brothers for this opportunity to be with you today as you celebrate your 100th Anniversary since the founding of your society. This is proof of your desire to be in communion with the Successor of Peter, the Holy Father Benedict the Sixteenth. As the representative of the Holy See here in Kenya I wish to thank the Maryknoll Society for your continual work in mission. I encourage you to explore new initiatives in pastoral work.

I would like to pay tribute to the early missionaries for their gallant missionary work among the local people in Kenya and in the rest of the African countries. These early missionaries did not know where they were going. They knew very little about culture. Cultures are in evolution. During these past 50 years in Eastern Africa we have seen many political and social changes. We have seen the shift from colonialism to independence. During this time the Catholic Church has made a great contribution to our society.

Unlike today, when we are living in the world of modern technology, the internet included, our early missionaries were moving from nowhere to new discoveries. They had nothing like the internet to guide them on where they were going. They wholly depended on their faith and belief.

Our mission is more than social promotion. We have to announce Jesus Christ. If we believe in the future we cannot be fixed in the past. The Mission of Jesus Christ is the future of humankind.

Three words for reflection: three words for real meditation

The importance of the **"Mission"** *ad gentes:*

- Necessity today, after 50 years, to start any Catholic reflection about the "Mission" going back to Vatican II.
- Importance to read – again and again – Vatican II, but in the context of today, considering the mission of Christ for the salvation of the World and Christ being the new Adam.
- Today, celebrating the centenary of Maryknoll, is an opportunity to meditate about the significance of what means to live our faith in the world where we are.

"Mission" of the Church in the "**Modern World.**" What "Modern world" mean?

I. What was the "Modern World" for the missionaries 100 years ago?

- To announce to all different peoples and continents.
- To go to the totally unknown world for ever.
- To meet so many cultures and to consider also the role that the missionary congregations played in the past for keeping the different cultures, initiating the study of the different languages and artworks.
- First confrontation of Christian Faith and Cultures.
- To consider culture not only as a static fact but as a human fact in evolution.

II. What was the "Modern World" for "Mission" 50 years ago in Africa?

- Context of the Decolonization.
- Context of the Independence.
- Africa is making the experience of its own responsibility
- The Catholic Church is present in the context of the decolonization and independence of Africa, and the particular Churches are

taking their responsibility in the spirit of Vatican II.

III. What is the "Modern World" for "Mission" today in Africa?

* Context of the "globalization."
* Africa and the globalized world.
* The Catholic Church in Africa and in the globalized modern world.
* The Universal Church in tension between:
  Subsidiarity: Diversity and
  Solidality: Unity.

In conclusion: The Catholic Teaching in a globalized world and in the context of Africa

* Evangelization of the cultures: true challenge of inculturation.
* Social teaching of the Church for Africa: formation of the lay people for assuming their responsibility.

His Grace Archbishop Allan Lebeaupin is the representative of the Holy See in Kenya and the Permanent Observer of the Holy See to UNEP (United Nations Environment Programme) and UN-HABITAT (United Nations Human Settlements Programme).

Concluding Remarks

Rev. Paul R. Masson, MM
Assistant General, Maryknoll Fathers and Brothers

It is an honor to represent the Maryknoll Fathers and Brothers at this Mission Symposium at Tangaza College. I have been very impressed by the participation of so many young men and women and their interest in the future of Mission, in African and from Africa. Also, it is a sign of hope to see the participation of the different Religious and Mission organizations. We are in a very important time for Mission, for Evangelization, in the world.

As members of the Maryknoll Fathers and Brothers, the Catholic Foreign Mission Society of America, we are completing 100 years as a Society, and 65 years in Africa. There have been many changes in our understanding of the Mission of the Church in last 100 years. There is a need for humility, to recognize our mistakes and shortcomings. Also, there is need to recognize the graces that we have received from the people of Asia, Africa and Latin America.

I have had the opportunity of living and participating in the Church of Latin America, in Chile and in Mexico. In their Concluding Document of the V General Conference of the Bishops of Latin America and the Caribbean, in Aparecida, Brazil, 13-31 May, 2007, the Bishops of Latin America remind us that the Church's mission is to evangelize and that all baptized Christians are called to be Disciples of Jesus Christ and are called to participate in the Mission of Jesus Christ.

Paragraph 209 reads: "The laity are 'by baptism made one body with Christ and are constituted among the People of God; they are in their own way made sharers in the priestly, prophetical, and kingly functions of Christ; and they carry our for their own part the mission of the whole Christian people in the Church and in the world (Lumen 31').["]1

It is a challenge for our Church to search for ways that all of us, as Brothers and Sisters, can realize our gifts and services to realize a world of Justice, Peace, and Harmony in our beautiful earth.

Thank you for this opportunity to listen to your insights and reflections. Thank you for the gracious hospitality here at Tangaza.

---

1   V General Conference of the Bishops of Latin America and the Caribbean, Aparecida. Published by with permission in the United States by the US Conference of Catholic Bishops, 3211 Fourth Street, NE, Washington, DC 20017-1194 .

Rev. Paul R. Masson, M.M., currently serves as an Assistant General for the Maryknoll Fathers and Brothers Leadership Council, New York, USA. He served as Pastor of La Virgen de la Luz Parish in Ciudad Juarez, Chihuahua, Mexico where he lived for over 10 years while serving as a member of the Maryknoll Mission Border Team. He holds a Master of Divinity degree from Maryknoll Seminary, Ossining, N.Y. (1972) and a bachelor's degree in philosophy from Maryknoll College, Glen Ellyn, Ill. (1965).

Concluding Remarks

Most Rev. Boniface Lele, Archbishop of Mombasa, Kenya

I congratulate the Maryknoll Society for your 100 years of missionary work, and thank you for your commitment and dedication as pastoral agents in Africa and indeed in the whole world. I would also like to thank the early missionaries from Europe and North America who came to Kenya to plant the church during the hard times when there was widespread malaria, poor or non-existent roads, and difficult living conditions.

I got into contact with the Maryknoll through Father Joe Trainor and Brother Frank TenHoopen, who used to give me accommodation whenever I visited my late brother who used to stay in Tudor in Mombasa. When I took over as the Archbishop of Mombasa Archdiocese in 2005, I started working with Brother Frank as the Youth Coordinator. Later I appointed him as the Archdiocesan Procurator.

I would like to mention a number of projects that had been initiated by Maryknoll. These include:

"The Grandsons of Abraham" that is currently being run by the Sisters of St. Joseph.

The project for people with HIV/AIDS that was run by the late Brother John Mullen – a volunteer community-based, home-based healthcare apostolate. The volunteer healthcare workers, known as Wahudumu wa Afya, are now spread in most of the parishes in our Central and Western deaneries.

The presence of Dr. Susan Nagele and Mary Oldham in our Archdiocese further strengthens our relationship with Maryknoll.

Maryknoll also has been assisting the Archdiocese in terms of sponsorship. I would like to introduce Brother John Nderitu, who is a student in Tangaza, as one of the beneficiaries.

Another example of our collaboration with Maryknoll is the Pastoral Centre in Tudor.

Now to our theme – "The Future of Mission in Africa." A new shift is being witnessed today. Christianity is growing at a higher rate in the Southern Hemisphere compared to the Northern Hemisphere. Religious vocations are dwindling in the Northern Hemisphere while they were increasing very fast in the Southern Hemisphere. Hence there is the possibility for the Catholic Church in Africa to send missionaries to the Northern Hemisphere. Yes, African missionaries can re-evangelize Europe and North America.

In this process we continue to learn from one another and to share with each other. Specifically, we can work together to promote the Catholic Church's involvement in justice and peace concerns.

Now, I am happy to close this mission symposium and to encourage you all in your missionary vocations. May the blessing of Almighty God descend upon you and remain with you forever. Amen.

NOTE: This speech was preceded by Simon Rurinjah, a Kenyan lay evangelist and good friend of Maryknoll for many years, reading a passage from the Gospel of St. *John* including Jesus's missionary mandate in *John* 20:21: "As the Father sends me I send you."

Archbishop Boniface Lele is the curent Bishop of the Catholic Archdiocese of Mombasa.

Contributors

Archbishop Allan Lebeaupin, The Apostolic Nuncio
Augustine Sawadogo
Archbishop Boniface E. Lele
Connie Martinon (Dr)
Edith Chamwama, MIAS BOOKS Editorial Staff
Emmanuel Manyasa (Dr)
Felix Ngao (Mr), CLM
Francis Kimani (Mr)
Joseph Healey (Rev), MM
John Conway (Rev), MM
Kathy Dunford (Mrs), MLM
Kenneth Thesing (Rev), MM
Lance Nadeau (Rev), MM
Laurenti Magesa (Rev)
Mary Oldham (Ms), MLM
Michael Kirwen (Rev), MM
Patrick Mwania (Rev), CSSp
Patrick Roe (Rev), CSSp
Paul Masson (Rev), MM
Peter Nyongesa (Rev)
Philomena Mwaura (Dr)
Teresa Hougnon Ougnon (Sr), MM
Sia Temu (Sr), MM